Accounting, Capitalism and the Revealed Religions

Vassili Joannidès de Lautour

Accounting, Capitalism and the Revealed Religions

A Study of Christianity, Judaism and Islam

palgrave
macmillan

Vassili Joannidès de Lautour
Grenoble École de Management
Grenoble, France

ISBN 978-3-319-32332-9 ISBN 978-3-319-32333-6 (eBook)
DOI 10.1007/978-3-319-32333-6

Library of Congress Control Number: 2016956215

Printed on acid-free paper

This Palgrave Macmillan imprint is published by Springer Nature
The registered company is Springer International Publishing AG Switzerland
The registered company address is: Gewerbestrasse 11, 6330 Cham, Switzerland

To Rachael, Rebecca and Clément

Foreword

This book is the conclusion of a comprehensive research project commenced in 2005 with a triple master's degree in in Social Sciences, Accounting & Finance and Education, followed by a PhD on accountability in a church setting.

This book owes its finalising to all those who have supported the research project from its earliest stage. Amongst them are all authors still alive cited in this book. They were all sent earlier versions of the PhD dissertation, the articles to be published in academic journals and other working papers that have fed this book. They were asked to articulate any comments on what was written, so that its contents would reflect as fairly as possible what their initial intent was at the time of their own studies. I met with all of them on numerous occasions. These insights were collected through tape-recorded interviews and written commentaries from the authors. These exchanges revolved around discussing how they decided to work on accounting and religion. Over years, some have become colleagues, co-authors and friends. As a result of all these privileged exchanges with such key authors, this book is the result of first-hand material.

Initially, the various chapters of this book were derived from a PhD dissertation. Some were presented and discussed at numerous conferences, including Interdisciplinary Perspectives on Accounting, Asia-Pacific Interdisciplinary Research in Accounting and the European Accounting Association. Chapter 6, dealing with accountability in the Salvation

Army, explicitly derives from the dissertation. In this respect, excerpts from interviews and anecdotes reported in this book were collected with informants' knowledge and consent. As with the authors cited in this work, informants were sent prior versions of the book's contents and were asked to make comments on them. In order for Salvation Army members to recognise their organisation's day-to-day life and activities more objectively, I purposefully changed their names. In so doing, I was allowing that people who were necessarily in the reported event incidentally could recognise themselves anyway. This process has two merits. Firstly, informants would approve any reference to them. Secondly, they would more broadly validate study plausibility by acknowledging it as authentic and true.

In its very essence, the topic borrows from several disciplines with different traditions and approaches to research. In this book, I have endeavoured systematically to refer to the home discipline of each topic discussed. Those are the philosophy of religion, the sociology of religion, economic philosophy, history of economic thought and accounting.

Special thanks to Nicolas Berland, Trevor Hopper, Danture Wickramasinghe, Anthony Berry, Eve Chiapello, John McKernan and Lee Parker.

Contents

List of Figures

1

Introduction

In this introduction, the book's key constructs are defined and put in perspective. These relate to accounting and accountability on one hand and to religion on the other. Accounting is understood as any means, including technologies, aimed at balancing debits and credits, while accountability is perceived as the giving and demanding of reasons for conduct, using any form of accounts. Religion appears as a threefold phenomenon: an individual encounter with the holy, witness to it before others and within a community of beliefs and practices. These definitions borrow both from the philosophy and sociology of religion and from accounting. The impetus behind this book derives from the intersection of these three notions.

In *Soll und Haben* (*Debit and Credit*), a novel published in Germany by Gustav Freytag in 1855, the main characters are a Protestant industrious family and a Jewish banking family, both developing capitalistic partnerships. Their mercantile relations are moralised by books of accounts. Both the Protestant and the Jew see God's benevolence in the accumulation of capital. Moreover, both *paters* write any business transactions in a book of accounts. This book is the Protestant's and the Jew's most personal item, their very intimacy. Hence, no one is authorised to even look at it. Later in Freytag's novel, the opening of the book of accounts reflects records regarding individual everyday actions (Freytag 1855; Maltby 1997). The Jew and the Protestant, in their capitalistic partnership, conducted 'eternal

V. Joannidès de Lautour, *Accounting, Capitalism and the Revealed Religions*, DOI 10.1007/978-3-319-32333-6_1

bookkeeping—and the act of accounting is for [them] a way of monitoring [their] moral as well as [their] financial position' (Maltby 1997, p. 78). In this book, it appears that Judaism and Protestantism, capitalism and double-entry bookkeeping conflate. In Freytag's novel, the spirit of capitalism pervades the morale of both the Jew and the Protestant.

The notion of religion will be used to determine any of the three religions revealed in the book. When those religions significantly differ, they are called Roman Catholicism, Judaism, Protestantism or Islam. So doing is by no means to dismiss non-monotheistic religions, but such a restriction conveniently allows the comparison of issues that emerged and developed coincidentally across time and space (Quattrone and Hopper 2005). The three monotheisms have expanded throughout the Indo-European continent since the Middle Ages.

It is my hope that this book can do justice to Freytag's novel by considering that capitalism is 'an imperative to unlimited accumulation of capital by formally peaceful means' (Boltanski and Chiapello 2006, p. 4). This implies economic rationality, efficiency, monetary exchange and calculations directed at profit-seeking (see Sombart 1911, p. 113; Chiapello 2007, pp. 266–267). This book explores connections between the three revealed monotheisms, the spirit of capitalism and essence of accounting. As the connections between capitalism and accounting have already been established (Bryer 1993; Carruthers and Espeland 1991; Chiapello 2007; Miller and Napier 1993), this point will not be discussed. Since this book's core interest lies in exploring the connections between accounting and religion, the links between capitalism and monotheism will only be elicited as a reminder.

Social scientists and humanists interested in the spirit of capitalism have connected it to the development of religion (Aqbal and Mirakhor 2006; Carruthers and Espeland 1991; Sombart 1911; Taqi-Usmani 2002; Weber 1921, 1922), with the discussion revolving around the influence of one or another religion on capitalism. Notwithstanding these debates, this book assumes that each of the four relevant religions has contributed in its way to the spirit of capitalism and relatedly to the development of accounting. Hence, neither just Protestantism nor only Christianity are being exposed and discussed.

In order to reveal the core links between accounting and religion, this introductory chapter provides a working definition of both accounting and religion. Central to this book, each of those two notions is defined as in its respective home discipline. Accounting is defined as per recommendations from sociology and economics, whilst religion's definition lies at the crossroads of sociology, anthropology and philosophy.

1 Accounting as a Rational and Systematic Practice

> (1) There is a *plan* in accordance with which all things are ordered aright. And the plan covers activities in the distant future. (2) *Efficiency* is the test applied in the choice of all the means of production. (3) Seeing that the 'cash nexus' regulates all economic activity, and that everywhere and always a surplus is sought for, exact *calculations* become necessary in every undertaking (Sombart 1911, p. 113).

1.1 Accounting as the Balancing of Debits and Credits

This chapter seeks to approach an ontology of accounting by exploring its ancient roots, which are assumed to be found in the revealed religions. Under this purview, accounting is deliberately decontextualised from the settings in which it is practiced. In other words, accounting's skeleton and soul are exposed, hence the reader understands how its very essence can be understood and observed. So doing follows McKernan's and Kosmala's (2007) deconstructionist approach to both accounting and religion, that is an approach consisting of depolluting these difficult notions of any contextual features. So doing is an exercise in simplification. Adjunct to the need for simplifying religion, accounting is also understood here in its simplest form largely agreed upon in academe: a process driven by a worldview resulting in categorising any situation into two, always equalling each other (Gambling 1987; Hopwood 1994; Weber 1922). Accounting research labels these two counterparts debits and credits (Maltby 1997).

Here, accounting is broadly understood as the logic of categorising conduct as liabilities (credit) and actions (debit) (Gallhofer and Haslam 1991; Gambling 1977, 1985, 1987; Hopwood 1994). Indeed 'the language of accounting has entered organizational and political discourses. We even have become accustomed to talk about ourselves in terms of assets, liabilities, resources and balances, and as we have, the possibilities for action have sometimes changed quite radically' (Hopwood 1994, p. 299).

It is now well established in the literature that accounting's birth and development have been concomitant to capitalism (Bryer 1993; Carruthers and Espeland 1991; Chiapello 2007; Miller and Napier 1993). Double-entry bookkeeping in particular and variations of accounting seem to have been presented as the recording of economic transactions (Bhimani 1994) under the patronage of the capital account, as defined by Weber (1921). No other rationale for accounting has been envisaged, except in social and environmental accounting (Gray 2002).

Although accounting is presented as a social and organisational practice, it is usually disconnected from its deeper roots, its religious foundations being thereby obscured. However, numerous theologians, philosophers and sociologists of religions have acknowledged the religious roots of accounting. In particular, in the Western world, they have long highlighted the role played by a Catholic monk, Luca Paccioli, in the development and expansion of double-entry bookkeeping, in the form of a systematisation and rationalisation of monks' day-to-day activities and monastery management (Aho 2005; Thompson 1991).

The core of accounting lies in identifying gifts received for a purpose and the use made thereof. In essence, debits and credits equal each other. The central issue is to be found in the identification of the right(eous) use of a gift. Accounting research tends to consider that the balancing of credits and debits can only be observed through formal representations, that is written records and books of accounts, with the items to be accounted for named first and then transformed into numbers through working units reflecting what should be balanced. Evaluation models and assumptions underlying the keeping of records reveal this. The formal representation offered by books of accounts serves to show that gifts were righteously used.

1.2 Accounting as Means of Accountability

The rationale for deeds is expected to be clarified to others with fairness, the speaker being held to an 'absolute obligation to the Other' (McKernan and Kosmala 2004, p. 356). His or her story finds itself 'held to be understandable to others and thereby [rendering] a life intelligible and meaningful' (Shearer 2002, p. 545). Religious notions of justness and fairness imply that the accountable self is constructed as a moral and responsible person seeking to speak the truth and expecting the Other to have faith in him or her (McKernan and Kosmala 2007).

Accounting cannot be understood regardless of the goal to which it is pursuant: accountability to a Higher-Principal (Joannidès 2012; Roberts and Scapens 1985). The balancing of debits and credits is indeed a means of the compulsory ability to give a fair account of one's activities and conduct. In this relation of 'giving and demanding of reasons for conduct' (Roberts and Scapens 1985, p. 447), the subject is constituted as answerable, in other words as one compulsorily able to give evidence of the reasonableness of his or her actions to a community of others. His or her accounts are 'held to be understandable to others and thereby [render] a life intelligible and meaningful' (Shearer 2002, p. 545).

The need to identify the person to whom one is accountable emphasises the fact that the demanding of accounts can be issued by an Other deemed legitimate to do so. In organisational contexts, legitimacy is granted to those who entrust resources to others for specific purposes and expect others to use such resources efficiently (Ahrens and Chapman 2002; Roberts and Scapens 1985; Schweiker 1993; Shearer 2002). The best-known resources are financial but these can be of a different nature. For instance, a soup kitchen can be entrusted soup cans whose use must be accounted for and reported to donors. In a religious setting, God entrusts human beings with a soul and conscience. The righteous use thereof is to be reported to this particular donor. Accordingly, these Higher-Stakeholders—that is, those who entrust resources to others—demand accounts proving the appropriateness of resource use to create value (Laughlin 1996).[1]

[1] Depending on the institution, the Higher-Stakeholder can be the community of shareholders (private companies), capital markets (listed companies), donors (registered charities) or taxpaying citizens (public sector organisations).

The content of these accounts answers the 'for what' question of accountability. In a world dominated by economic ideologies, the accountable self must give evidence of its commitment to creating financial value for stockholders (Shearer 2002, pp. 565–566). In reaction to neoclassical economists (e.g. Jensen) who restrict value to monetary surpluses,[2] proponents of welfare economics (e.g. Sen) broaden the notion to include social and environmental dimensions (Gray 2002, 2010).[3] From being strictly functional, accountability has evolved to embrace social and environmental aspects (O'Dwyer and Unerman 2007).

It is no secret that measuring value relies heavily on the calculative dimension of accounting.[4] Numerical figures give a visual, memorisable representation of resources and their use to create value. However, such numbers do not suffice to provide an understanding of what has been undertaken and why. Consequently, they are coupled with words that, at worst, label them and, at best, make sense of them (Quattrone 2004, pp. 657–658, 2009, p. 86). In sum, while numbers and calculations are used to record conduct and value, words serve to convey an intelligible story. Such is the case in annual reports where balance sheets, profit-and-loss accounts and cash flow statements presenting business activities in financial terms are complemented with texts explaining strategy, operations and future projects and prospects (McKernan and Kosmala 2004, p. 342). Likewise, in face-to-face meetings with investors, comments on numerical figures are demanded from accountable managers: questions are asked and satisfactory answers are expected (Roberts et al. 2006). Narrative accountability is directed at those who listen to and believe in (accounting) stories. For this reason, the speaker is held to an 'absolute obligation to the Other' (McKernan and Kosmala 2004, p. 356): he or she should tell a fair story of commitment to creating value that would be intelligible to any interested party.

---

[2] For these economists, the absence of maximisation functions makes non-financial accountability irrelevant.

[3] For instance, social value can be the welfare produced for society in general or specific parts of it. One measure of environmental value can be reductions in greenhouse gas emissions.

[4] To explain how calculations dominate accountability discourse, Quattrone (2004) shows how monks in the Society of Jesus used to quantify the lives of their flock. They accounted for souls through sacraments, sins and subsequent indulgences. These were valued at a price set by the clergy to remit offences against God.

Although the notion of accounting is generally understood as any form of account giving, this book will reduce it to double-entry bookkeeping and the balancing of debits and credits. Pursuant to the notion that accounting is a twin to capitalism and therefore the recording of economic transactions, financial evaluation of counterparties has colonised accounting. It is relatively convenient to have money as a commonly understood unit. Studying accounting in functional contexts prevents the use of units other than money (Berry 2005; Quattrone 2004, 2009). Accordingly, in order to approach accounting's very essence and ontology, it is necessary to depart from mere economic transactions and rather focus on the meaning of giving an account (McKernan and Kosmala 2004, 2007). From this angle, double-entry bookkeeping will leave money aside so as to focus on what seems to be central to accounting and religion.

2 Religion as the Linking of People

Too often, religion, theology and church institutions are amalgamated, thereby resulting in the core of *re-ligere* being ill-defined and misunderstood. Etymologically, religion is what links people through an individual encounter with the holy, the need to gather and share this with others and ultimately the issuance of orders and regulations for the community thence constituted (Derrida and Wieviorka 2001; Durkheim 1898; Eliade 1959; Latour 2002; Lévinas 1974, 1975; Weber 1922).

2.1 Religion as an Individual Encounter

The embracing of religion consists of an intimate, personal and subjective experience of the divine (Badiou 2003; Lévinas 1974, 1975). By essence, the latter is beyond the self and can be neither known nor approached. Accordingly, the individual can only speculate that he actually experienced the divine. Durkheim (1898) notes that such an experience can stem either from the observation of extraordinary events or from the need for a systematic explanation of the world. Durkheim notes the first assumption as follows:

> A notion that is generally considered as a feature of religious matters is that of supernatural. Thereby, one means any kind of thing that overcomes our understanding; supernatural is the world of mystery, non-knowledgeable, non-understandable. Hence, religion would be a sort of speculation on everything that science and more generally thinking do not explain (Durkheim 1898, p. 33).

For Durkheim, the second assumption is likely more convincing and more systematic. It can therefore apply to a large body of people.

> For, religious conceptions first of all purport to express and to explain, not extraordinary and abnormal events, but on the contrary continuity and regularity. Very generally, gods less give account of monstrosities, bizarre facts, abnormalities, than of the usual work of the universe, of the movement of planets, of the annual growth of plants, of the reproduction of species, etc. (Durkheim 1898, p. 39)

Seemingly, religion often commences with the experience of extraordinary events, which ask for explanation. This can be the case of a terminally ill person expecting death who miraculously recovers. If ordinary explanations fail, the individual may then seek for supernatural reasons. However, the premier experience of the divine is generally not to be explained. Seen from another perspective outside of the self, it does not necessarily look divine. Therefore, Durkheim considers that the qualification of divine experience by the individual itself suffices for the characterisation of religion. The divine experience is assimilated into the existence of supernatural forces and spirits wherewith the individual is connected or whereon he is dependent. It is:

> the determination of human life by the feeling of a linkage binding the human mind to the mysterious spirit. The former recognises the domination of the former over the world and itself and likes feeling united to it (Durkheim 1898, p. 40).

These supernatural spirits are 'determined by the nature that they are granted' (Durkheim 1898, p. 41).

As the individual believes in the existence of these supernatural spirits, nobody may either doubt or contest these beliefs. It is how individual faith is constructed. The self reposes the complete confidence in those spirits upon spiritual apprehension and not on proof. Faithfulness then is the constant, steadfast and systematic belief in the capabilities of these spirits. In brief, faithfulness overlaps with the systematic explanation of the world order. From then on, faithfulness can be disconnected from divinities, insofar as the individual relies on a satisfactory explanation of the world order. 'Even within deist religions, one can find a large amount of rites that are totally independent upon any idea of gods or of spiritual beings' (Durkheim 1898, p. 47).

2.2 Religion as Community

As a social community, a religion is 'not only a sacerdotal brotherhood; it is the moral community constructed by all believers of the same faith, laypeople as well as priests' (Durkheim 1898, p. 63). These are regarded as laypeople, parishioners or churchgoers. They gather on the basis of similar experiences and conceptions of divinity (Durkheim 1898; Weber 1922). The assembly of believers determines the number of gods as well as their characteristics. These latter broadly consist of their physical representation, if any, and of the scope of their supernatural capabilities (Durkheim 1898). Thirdly, believers adhere to the language and appropriate procedures for communicating with the divine body. For Weber and Durkheim, the divine language consists of prayers and praise. The procedures employed for praying and praising are the rites and the liturgy of the religious group. The liturgy is the usual procession of events in the course of worship. It makes the believers' conduct predictable and conveys systematic practices. Rites make conduct predictable outside the moment of worship. They are similar to liturgy at other times.

The religious community sets the boundaries of the sacred sanctuary and reciprocally defines the profane and the mundane (Durkheim 1898; Eliade 1959). Anything linked to deities is regarded as sacred. In particular, the premises where they are praised and prayed to shape the sacred sanctuary. Believers conduct themselves as wardens of the Sacred Sanctuary. Eliade notes:

> For the religious person, *space is not homogenous*; it evidences discontinuities, ruptures: there are parts of space that are qualitatively different from others. On the contrary, for profane experiences, space is homogenous and neutral: no discontinuity qualitatively differentiates its various parts (Eliade 1959, pp. 25–26).

These sacred places form the premises of the church building, as Eliade further argues:

> In order to point out the non-homogeneity of space, as experienced by the religious person, one can refer to a banal example: a church building, in a contemporary city. For the believer, that church is part of another space than the street where it is located. The gate that opens to the interior conveys a form of continuity. The threshold that separates both spaces conveys at the same time the distance between both modes of being: profane and religious. The threshold is at the same time the boundary that differentiates both worlds, and the paradoxical place where both worlds communicate, where one can move from the profane world to the sacred world (Eliade 1959, p. 28).

Two religious issues stem from Eliade's note. First, it is to have a sanctuary, that is a place where the religious moment can take place. Secondly, it is to preserve it in its sacred condition. Hence, religion encompasses the places where devotees may share their religious experiences with other believers. They then become churchgoers, as they go to the church building for that purpose. The collection of church buildings devoted to the same deities then forms the Church (Schoenherr 1987; Weber 1922). When attending one or another church building, believers are considered to be parishioners. The label employed for the characterisation of believers informs one about the nature of their religion. If only believers, they are in an individualistic scheme. If they are churchgoers, religion has become collective and has erected a sacred sanctuary. If they are parishioners, religion is institutionalised and has several affiliates. In brief, the term employed informs about the degree of institutionalisation of a religion and also its spatial scope. When institutionalised, the religious community becomes a congregation, which 'arises in connection with a prophetic movement as a result of routinization' (Weber 1922, p. 452).

A religion can operate within a denomination, in other words like a church within the church. A religious denomination is a sub-movement within a broader Church (Brinkerhoff 1978; Luidens 1982; Pearson 1969). The denomination shares the same religious objectives as the church, although local objectives and ways and means for the accomplishment of the church project may vary (Brinkerhoff 1978). Accordingly, numerous different denominations can operate under the same church label. Roman Catholicism admits various denominations, like the Benedictines, the Franciscans, the Opus Dei, the Immanuel and so on. Similarly, Protestantism operates as a meta-label for numerous denominations, like Reformed, Lutherans, Calvinists, Methodists, Baptists, Anabaptists, Evangelists and the rest. Denominations borrow characteristics from sects, inasmuch as people adhere to the project without necessarily being born into them. In that context, the Church is a confederation of local congregations and denominations.

2.3 Religion as Doctrines

As Weber (1922, p. 1164) notes, an institutionalised religion relies on a clergy. These people have a specific status in the organisation. They are vocational priests. In the capacity of a religious elite, they work full-time at establishing contact with the deities and on coaching their flock. Their status makes them live differently from churchgoers. For instance, priests in the Roman Catholic Church stay single and may not have children. Together, the members of the clergy manage the religious belief system (Durkheim 1898, 1902; Eliade 1959; Weber 1922), which shapes the specificity of the religious community. It encompasses the identity of deities (characteristics and capabilities), the significant rites and the meaning of myths and symbols. In fact, it is a system that aligns with the beliefs. It codifies what is appropriate and what is not, as well as good and evil, holy and ugly/blasphemy, sacred and profane, and so forth. It offers interpretation of the deities' will and expectations through the understanding of symbols. In one sense, members of the clergy tell the truth of the religious community in the religious belief system (Ricœur 1991). Correlatively, clergy members are legitimate for punishing any deviant conduct.

It is the religious elite that codifies beliefs. For Weber, such collective codification requires systematic and standardised procedures. These form the theology of the community (Derrida and Wieviorka 2001; Latour 2002).

Etymologically, theology is the science of God. Accordingly, clergy members are scientists of God. Hence, they are identified as knowledgeable of Him and His essence. By studying His utterances and realisations, they can understand and know Him. In that capacity, they may intermediate between the believers and the deities. For Latour, theology, like other sciences, has recourse to systematic devices. Like scientists, theologians model and represent deities. If they do not do it on their own, they order it from others. Theologians are hidden behind such scientific methods that ipso facto are not to be contested; the universal laws that can be drawn mechanically apply without argument. This is one step on the way to the domination of the community. Indeed, these scientific-religious laws predict gods' reactions to given human conduct. In brief, theologians supposedly know what is good or evil, ugly or holy, sacred or blasphemy… Thus, their knowledge of God allows that they lead the religious community.

The religious elite (Weber 1922) or the clergy (Durkheim 1898, 1902), dominates the community by administering the religious belief system. In fact, their power stems from their special knowledge of divinity. According to the religious community, theologians may have responded to a calling or may have been selected personally by God. In either case, they have notably been in contact with deities. In that capacity, they have been able to operate as intermediaries between gods and mankind. Despite scientific claims, theology is a hermeneutic work on deities (Ricœur 1991).[5] Different conclusions or methods for the interpretation of the gods result in various approaches, that is various theologies. Even within one community several theologies may exist. Either they all converge and coexist within the same premises, or they do not and therefore exist separately. Separation may result in the constitution of new independent churches or in the constitution of new denominations within the existing church.[6] In brief, to each denomination corresponds to its own way of conceiving, praying to and praising the deities, in other words: one theology.

[5] Consistently with these views on theology, the present study positions itself in a hermeneutic scheme.

[6] This book will not address issues in the construction of official theology. It will deliberately leave aside strategy issues as well as theological disputes. It will position itself after choices were made and will not discuss them.

Bibliography

Aho, J. (2005). *Confession and bookkeeping—The religious, moral, and rhetorical roots of modern accounting*. New York: State University of New York Press.

Ahrens, T., & Chapman, C. S. (2002). The structuration of legitimate performance measures and management: Day-to-day contests of accountability in a U.K. restaurant chain. *Management Accounting Research, 13*(2), 151–171.

Aqbal, Z., & Mirakhor, A. (2006). *Introduction to Islamic finance: Theory and practice*. London: John Wiley & Sons.

Badiou, A. (2003). *Saint Paul: The foundation of universalism*. Stanford, CA: Stanford University Press.

Berry, A. (2005). Accountability and control in a cat's cradle. *Accounting Auditing and Accountability Journal, 18*(2), 255–297.

Bhimani, A. (1994). Accounting and the emergence of 'economic man'. *Accounting Organizations and Society, 19*(8), 637–674.

Boltanski, L. et Chiapello, E. (2006). *The new spirit of capitalism*. London: Verso.

Brinkerhoff, M. B. (1978). Religion and goal orientations: Does denomination make a difference? *Sociological Analysis, 39*(3), 203–218.

Bryer, R. A. (1993). Double-entry bookkeeping and the birth of capitalism: Accounting for the commercial revolution in Medieval Northern Italy. *Critical Perspectives on Accounting, 4*(2), 113–140.

Carruthers, B. G., & Espeland, W. N. (1991). Accounting for rationality: Double-entry bookkeeping and the rhetoric of economic rationality. *The American Journal of Sociology, 97*(1), 31–69.

Chiapello, E. (2007). Accounting and the birth of the notion of capitalism. *Critical Perspectives on Accounting, 18*(3), 263–296.

Derrida, J., & Wieviorka, M. (2001). *Foi et savoir*. Paris: Seuil.

Durkheim, E. (1898). *The elementary forms of religious life*. Oxford: Oxford's World's Classics.

Durkheim, E. (1902). *Division of labour in society*. London: Free Press.

Eliade, M. (1959). *The sacred & the profane–The nature of religion—The significance of religious myth, symbolism, ritual within life and culture*. San Diego, CA: Harcourt Brace Jovanovich.

Freytag, G. (1855). *Soll und Haben*. Berlin: Weichert.

Gallhofer, S., & Haslam, J. (1991). The aura of accounting in the context of a crisis: Germany and the First World War. *Accounting Organizations and Society, 16*(5–6), 487–520.

Gambling, T. (1977). Magic, accounting and morale. *Accounting Organizations and Society, 2*(2), 141–151.
Gambling, T. (1985). The accountant's guide to the Galaxy, including the profession at the end of the Universe. *Accounting Organizations and Society, 10*(4), 415–425.
Gambling, T. (1987). Accounting for rituals. *Accounting Organizations and Society, 12*(4), 319–329.
Gray, R. (2002). The social accounting project and accounting organizations and society privileging engagement, imaginings, new accountings and pragmatism over critique? *Accounting Organizations and Society, 27*(7), 687–708.
Gray, R. (2010). Is accounting for sustainability actually accounting for sustainability … and how would we know? An exploration of narratives of organisations and the planet. *Accounting, Organizations and Society, 35*(1), 47–62.
Hopwood, A. G. (1994). Accounting and everyday life: An introduction. *Accounting Organizations and Society, 19*(3), 299–301.
Joannidès, V. (2012). Accounterability and the problematics of accountability. *Critical Perspectives on Accounting, 23*(3), 244–257.
Latour, B. (2002). *Jubiler—ou les tourments de la parole religieuse*. Paris: Seuil.
Laughlin, R. (1996). Principals and higher-principals: Accounting for accountability in the caring professions. In R. Munro & J. Mouritsen (Eds.), *Accountability: Power, ethos and the technologies of managing* (pp. 225–244). London: International Thomson Business Press.
Lévinas, E. (1974). *Otherwise than being or beyond essence*. Pittsburgh, PA: Duquesne University Press.
Lévinas, E. (1975). *God, death and time*. Stanford, CA: Stanford Univeristy Press.
Luidens, D. A. (1982). Bureaucratic control in a Protestant denomination. *Journal for the Scientific Study of Religion, 21*(2), 163–175.
Maltby, J. (1997). Accounting and the soul of the middle-class: Gustav Freytag's *Soll und Haben*. *Accounting Organizations and Society, 22*(1), 69–87.
McKernan, J. F., & Kosmala, K. (2004). Accounting, love and justice. *Accounting Auditing and Accountability Journal, 17*(3), 327–360.
McKernan, J. F., & Kosmala, K. (2007). Doing the truth: Religion—Deconstruction—Justice, and accounting. *Accounting Auditing and Accountability Journal, 20*(5), 729–764.
Miller, P., & Napier, C. (1993). Genealogies of calculation. *Accounting Organizations and Society, 18*(7–8), 631–647.
O'Dwyer, B., & Unerman, J. (2007). From functional to social accountability: Transforming the accountability relationship between funders and

non-governmental development organisations. *Accounting Auditing and Accountability Journal, 20*(3), 446–471.

Pearson, S. C. J. (1969). From church to denomination: American congregationalism in the nineteenth century. *Church History, 38*(1), 67–87.

Quattrone, P. (2004). Accounting for God: Accounting and accountability practices in the Society of Jesus (Italy, XVI–XVII centuries). *Accounting Organizations and Society, 29*(7), 647–683.

Quattrone, P. (2009). Books to be practiced: Memory, the power of the visual, and the success of accounting. *Accounting Organizations and Society, 34*(1), 85–118.

Quattrone, P., & Hopper, T. (2005). A 'time-space odyssey': Management control systems in two multinational organisations. *Accounting Organizations and Society, 30*(7–8), 735–764.

Ricœur, P. (1991). *Du texte à l'action*. Paris: Seuil.

Roberts, J., Sanderson, P., Barker, R., & Hendry, J. (2006). In the mirror of the market: The disciplinary effects of company/fund manager meetings. *Accounting Organizations and Society, 31*(3), 277–294.

Roberts, J., & Scapens, R. (1985). Accounting systems and systems of accountability—Understanding accounting practices in their organisational contexts. *Accounting Organizations and Society, 10*(4), 443–456.

Schoenherr, R. A. (1987). Power and authority in organized religion: Disaggregating the phenomenological core. *Sociological Analysis, 47*(Supp.), 52–71.

Schweiker, W. (1993). Accounting for ourselves: Accounting practices and the disclosure of ethics. *Accounting Organizations and Society, 18*(2–3), 231–252.

Shearer, T. (2002). Ethics and accountability: From the for-itself to the for-the-other. *Accounting Organizations and Society, 27*(6), 541–573.

Sombart, W. (1911). *The Jews and modern capitalism*. Kitchener, ON: Batoche Books Limited.

Taqi-Usmani, M. (2002). *An introduction to Islamic finance (Arab and Islamic laws)*. Boston, MA: CQ Press.

Thompson, G. (1991). Is accounting rhetorical? Methodology, Luca Pacioli and printing. *Accounting Organizations and Society, 16*(5–6), 572–599.

Weber, M. (1921). *The Protestant ethic and the spirit of capitalism*. New York: Routledge.

Weber, M. (1922). *Economy and society*. Berkeley: The University of California Press.

2

The Book and the Spirits of Capitalism

As it is commonly agreed that accounting and capitalism were born and have developed coincidentally, this chapter shows how each of the book's four religions has accompanied the advancement of capitalism. The chapter is grounded in the sociology of religions and rests its argument upon its major thinkers. Judaism has accompanied the development of merchants' capitalism and contemporary financial practices. Roman Catholicism has been at the origin of property management and estate promotion. Protestantism is the incarnation of the spirit of industrious capitalism. Lastly, Islam is the foundation of social capitalism. Once this is established the reader can easily understand how accounting is grounded in religion, which is further developed in Chap. 3.

It is commonly agreed that double-entry bookkeeping and capitalism were born and have evolved coevally (Bryer 2000a, b; Bryer 1993; Carruthers and Espeland 1991; Chiapello 2007; Derks 2008; Miller and Napier 1993). These works are very suggestive of Weber's argument that economic rationality needs a rational and systematic ordering of assets and liabilities, as in the account of capital (Weber 1922). As capitalism is not uniform and varies across cultures, space and time (Deeg 2009; Lane and Geoffrey 2009), one could wonder from which form of capitalism accounting originates. While accounting is presented as a way of keeping records of capitalistic operations, it is argued that books of accounts serve as moral practice within capitalism. As a moral device, accounting is argued to be influenced by religious

V. Joannidès de Lautour, *Accounting, Capitalism and the Revealed Religions*, DOI 10.1007/978-3-319-32333-6_2

thought underpinned by faith (Carruthers and Espeland 1991; Maltby 1997; McKernan and Kosmala 2004, 2007; McPhail and Walters 2009). In such a context, it is consistent and unsurprising that Lucca Pacioli and other merchants wrote on the bottom of their books of accounts 'in the name of God', to Whom they were addressed (Carruthers and Espeland 1991; Maltby 1997). This points to the question of whether books of accounts be kept for economic or religious reasons; it is therefore crucial to understand how religion has positioned itself vis-à-vis the spread of capitalism.

So doing is the condition under which this book's subsequent chapters can be understood. More specifically, this chapter delineates how each of the book's four religions have accompanied the development of a certain form of capitalism over centuries since the Middle Ages. That period is chosen here as it reflects a time of bitter theological debates and necessary interactions common to the four religions. This chapter, however, does not engage in such discussions but only focuses on how each religion has fostered a form of capitalism that has characterised it.

This endeavour borrows from the sociology of religions' main works and authors, although it would be judicious to proceed chronologically. The decision made here is to start with the most well-known ideas with regards to the Protestant ethic and the spirit of capitalism (Weber 1921). This necessarily leads us to continue with Sombart's (1911) discussion of Judaism's influence on capitalism. Then, borrowing from medievalists' economic systems, we discuss theologies and practices of the Roman Catholic Church, in reaction to Reformation. Lastly, Islam's economic theology is developed through the lens of Rodinson's (1966) work. It is now well-grounded in the sociology of capitalism that religions have played a major role in its development (Aqbal and Mirakhor 2006; Carruthers and Espeland 1991; Derks 2008; Gambling and Karim 1991; Rodinson 1966; Sombart 1911; Taqi-Usmani 2002; Weber 1921, 1922).

1 The Protestant Ethic and the Spirit of Capitalism

In Weber's (1921) study on the religious affiliation of German industry leaders, he observed that these tended to be Protestants rather than Catholics. He ascribed this statement to the Protestant ethic that encourages capitalistic undertaking and success. On the contrary, money and capital are taboos within Roman Catholicism. The following paragraphs highlight the core features of the Protestant ethic.

> Among journeymen [...] the Catholics show a stronger propensity to remain in their crafts, that is they more often become master craftsmen, whereas the Protestants are attracted to a larger extent into the factories in order to fill the upper ranks of skilled labour and administrative positions. The explanation of these cases is undoubtedly that the mental and spiritual peculiarities acquired from the environment, here the type of education favoured by the religious atmosphere and the parental home, have determined the choice of occupation, and through it the professional career (Weber 1921, p. 6).

The Reformation took place as a reaction to the Roman Catholic notion of divine grace and its delineations. To meet God's requirements, the individual must respond His calling, which consists of vocational work.

> One thing was unquestionably new: the valuation of the fulfilment of duties in worldly affairs as the highest form which the moral activity of the individual could assume. This it was which inevitably gave every-day worldly activity a religious significance, and which created the conception of calling in this sense (Weber 1921, p. 40).

The unique way to be pleasing to God is to do one's work as well as possible. Therefore, if the individual works well, God rewards him through the compensation that he receives. Only the self must seek to know what God decided and to preserve that confidence in Jesus Christ that results from actual faith: 'in practice, God helps those who help themselves' (p. 69).

Divine grace appears a priori: in practice, God helps those who help themselves. The self's responsibility is to accept or to refuse it. To accept it means that he will have to work hard to maintain it. Any personal gift is to be cultivated. It is that cultivation that rewards success. Symmetrically, this means that God approves the self's actions and undertakings. To do so, the individual has to understand what God has planned for him and to do it. Then, God will bless him.

> (1) [...] the methodical development of one's own state of grace to a higher and higher degree of certainty and perception in terms of the law was a sign of grace, and (2) [...] God's Providence works through those in such a state of perfection, i.e. in that He gives them His signs if they wait patiently and deliberate methodically. Labour in a calling was also the ascetic activity *par excellence* for A. H. Francke; that God Himself blessed His chosen ones through the success of their labours was [...] undeniable to him (p. 84).

God is not elitist, as He offers His grace for free under the sole condition that the self agrees to work on developing its gifts. By doing so, the self praises the Lord and manifests His glory on Earth. That is why God sends to every self an explicit signal, but if the self misses the occasion once it will not be rewarded. This is not a punishment—the individual is merely not yet saved. He will be once he accepts divine grace and Jesus Christ as saviour.

Education allows skilled labour and subsequently the accumulation of capital. As that form of rationality is the most explicit way of appraising success, Weber regards it as the most natural way of honouring God's blessings. The Protestant ethic then consists of thanking God for His blessings and of paying Him back by funding one's church. Faithfully, he pays back from the capital that he has accumulated by supporting his church financially. The Protestant ethic thus incarnates the spirit of capitalism of the industrious bourgeoisie.

2 Judaism and Modern Capitalism

Sombart (1911) challenges Weber by ascribing the spirit of Capitalism to Judaism rather than to Protestantism.[1]

[1] When first published in 1911, *The Jews and Modern Capitalism* was considered as a philo-Semitic book. Sombart endeavoured to explain how the exclusion of Jews from citizenship throughout Europe led them to construct their belonging to society on different bases. Nowadays, a few Jewish scholars regard Sombart's work in accordance with his later enrolment in National Socialism and take it as being anti-Semitic. The present chapter takes it as it was first intended, in other words regardless of Sombart's later political shift and engagement.

> For any one who followed them could not but ask himself whether all that Weber ascribes to Puritanism might not with equal justice be referred to Judaism, and probably in a greater degree; nay, it might well be suggested that which is called Protestantism is in reality Judaism (Sombart 1911, p. 134).

In his book, Sombart undertakes a historic explanation of the position of Jewish people in international capitalism. The spirit of capitalism lies in the context wherein Judaism has evolved throughout Europe. Initially, as Exodus states, the Jewish People have always been a wandering people. This has been manifested in the Europe-wide Jewish Diaspora. Jewish people have settled wherever they could have an occupation.

> One result of these wanderings was the off-shoots of one and the same family took root in different centres of economic life and established great world-famed firms with numerous branches in all parts (p. 119).

The dispersion of families facilitated the development of international trade, as visiting families were able to bring their overseas experiences and products to each other. For Sombart, it was likely that

> the Jews had at the very beginning—scattered centres from which to carry on international commerce and to utilize international credit; 'great correspondence' in short, the first necessity for all international organization (p. 120).

Since the Exodus, the Jewish People has been able to develop international trade and commercial organisations, that is international Capitalism.[2] Products could be developed in one country and sold in others. Sombart notes that the Jewish people became good at producing in cheap markets and selling in more lucrative ones. Likewise, the institutionalisation of trade has often resulted in companies establishing national branches. In the same vein, the distribution of goods became increasingly international.

---

[2] Nowadays, the new spirit of capitalism, as connected to globalisation, seems to do justice to Sombart's views. Globalisation consists of companies operating everywhere. It has become commonplace to deem international trade as a phenomenon of the twentieth century. In that respect, the new spirit of capitalism is much indebted to the history of the Jewish people and of Judaism.

As Jewish families were scattered throughout Europe and moved often from one country to another, they found themselves obliged to develop linguistic skills. Branches of a family would speak different languages. Hence, benefitting children, who would become multilingual. The broad spread of the Jewish diaspora has historically allowed the wider Jewish community to oversee a network of transportation companies in international ports and harbours. As a result, Jewish entrepreneurs have also been able to transport and oversee the production of raw material in mines and mills across the world. This network has not only generated capital over time, but has also allowed the Jewish business community to strengthen and develop on an international level, engendering further economic opportunity and success both within and outside of their immediate community.

Coincidentally with Christian prohibition of financial activities, only Jews were allowed to trade money. This encouraged some Jewish people to develop finance and banking activities in Europe. Accordingly, Sombart stresses

> The progress of the Jews to *la haute finance* was invariably as follows. In the first instance their linguistic ability enabled them to be of service to crowned heads as interpreters, then they were sent as intermediaries or special negotiators to foreign courts. Soon they were put in charge of their employer's fortunes, at the same time being honoured through his graciousness in allowing them to become his creditors. From this point it was no long step to the control of State finances, and in later years of the Stock Exchanges (p. 122).

This was the case where Jewish people were welcomed, especially in Holland and England, including those countries influenced by the Reformation. Contrary to some Latin countries, where they were only tolerated, here they were generally allowed solely to trade money, and in doing so they were taking over activities that Christian citizens were not allowed to do. Thereby, launching the first banks with revenues from trade activities, some Jewish people managed to become financial engineers and counsellors to monarchs and governments across Europe.

> This in fact was why Jewish wealth was so influential. It enabled capitalistic undertakings to be started, or at least facilitated the process. To establish banks, warehouses, stock and share-broking—all this was easier for the Jew

> than for the others because his pockets were better lined. That, too, was why he became banker to crowned heads. And finally, because he had money he was able to lend it. This activity paved the way for Capitalism to a greater degree than anything else did. For modern Capitalism is the child of money-lending. Money-lending contains the root of Capitalism [...] *In fine*, the characteristics of money-lending are the characteristics of all modern capitalistic economic organizations (pp. 132–133).

In Latin European countries, the status of Jews was more ambiguous as they were in some places only tolerated and concurrently they were both prosecuted and admired. As the spirit of capitalism has historically been embodied both by Protestantism and Judaism, it has not evolved independently from them. The Protestant ethic incarnates its principles, whereas Judaism incarnates its historical practical development. Given the Jewish roots of Protestantism, it is not surprising that Judaism developed capitalism in Protestant England and Holland. The rise of capitalism was strongly dependent upon the history of the Jewish people. Its spirit has then been institutionalised since the Reformation alongside the emergence of the industrial bourgeoisie in Germany, England and Holland. In Latin countries, the Roman Catholic Church left little space to Protestantism and Judaism. Nonetheless, these places too have expanded capitalistically since the Renaissance.

3 Renaissance Italy's Catholicism as the Spirit of Profitmaking

Most pieces of work on the spirit of capitalism note a further opposition of Sombart to Weber, insofar as the former would ascribe the spirit of capitalism to the Roman Catholic Church (Bryer 1993; Chiapello 2007; Miller and Napier 1993; Tinker 2004). Yet, money has always been absent in Catholic theologies (Derks 2008).[3] What historians of

[3] For instance, Franciscans have always argued that poverty would make people more attentive to religious matters. According to Franciscans, goods owners would be more concerned about shielding their property than about being pleasing to God. In the same vein, Benedictines have defended poverty. Once rid of any property, the individual is rid of any worry. He is able to study full-time God's words.

Catholicism have unanimously outlined is that the Church has operated like a capitalistic organisation since the Renaissance, either in France (Duby 1979; Michaud 1991) or in Italy (Hallman 1985).

> For most medievalists, the view that the Roman Catholic church energetically pursued its economic interests in competition with other participants in the market at the local, national and international level is standard knowledge (Derks 2008, p. 199).

When working on Catholic capitalism, they have mainly 'focused upon the venality of the church and particularly upon the fiscal practices of the Roman curia' (Hallman 1985, p. 1). The Roman Catholic Church has historically been driven by the accumulation of income. Purportedly, it has traded religious services, such as marriage (Davidson and Ekelund Jr. 1997), confession (Aho 2005) or more broadly the cure of souls (Hallman 1985). As churchgoers were to book their seat in Heaven, they were to pay for the perpetual cure of their soul, including the practice of marriage and confession of their sins. This is what Hallman characterises as an 'ecclesial benefice'.

> An ecclesial benefice is a sacred office, with or without the care of souls, to which a perpetual income is attached. By the end of the Middle Ages, church benefices had become the primary reservoir from which popes rewarded their servants. This system encouraged churchmen to view benefices first as income and only secondarily as sacred offices (Hallman 1985, p. 1).

Clearly, the accumulation of church income rested upon parishioners. These were to pay throughout their lives for religious services. Hence, each Christian was considered as a provisional provider of resources for the church. Therefore, every believer, as a source for funding, was recorded in the books of the Church (Quattrone 2009). This allowed provisioning them as accrued perpetual income until death.

> Provision of a benefice by the pope and the cardinals in consistory was only the first step in the accumulation of income (Hallman 1985, p. 19).

Such accrued income and provisions rest upon the Original Sin as the basis of Catholic theology. In fact, since Adam and Eve were excluded from Eden, mankind has been regarded as intrinsically sinning. As sinners, all believers would have to pay back for their sinner condition. Payments would address what makes sense to them on earth, for example monetary fees and fines. The absence of redemption and of self-justification in Roman Catholicism forced the self to pay back unto death. At the same time, missionaries got new people converted. The same rules have applied to newly converted people. The Roman Catholic Church has perpetually been able to accumulate financial resources.[4]

> These indulgences, whether granted for a single benefice or several [...] always cite a specific sum of money (Hallman 1985, p. 44).

These perpetual rents allowed that the Church acquired properties. These were then managed in order to generate additional income. Monies were perpetually reinvested in properties, and so forth. This is how the Roman Catholic Church has accumulated capital and constructed the largest fortune worldwide. The management of church property consisted of alienating them, in the form of letting or leasing vacancies and of receiving instalments as counterparts. Thereby, the Roman Catholic Church gave birth to estate capitalism.

> The assignment of monetary pensions from ecclesial property was not confined to benefices that had been in the pensioner's possession [...] Incomes from church benefices were used, then, as a matter of course, to support courtiers, both lay and ecclesiastical (Hallman 1985, pp. 52–53).

Simultaneously, Roman Catholicism has developed incentives-based capitalism. Properties could be distributed to reward faithful churchmen

---

[4] In Davidson's and Ekelund Jr.'s (1997) article, the theory of interest is metaphorically applied to the evaluation of provisional rents. The Church accounted for people from their birth unto their death. Its leaders had insights into the fecundity rate of couples and into mortality. They were able to know how many living children a couple would have. The rents from one couple could be multiplied by the expected amount of offspring and their ability to pay the same rent. In brief, to Michaud, the resources of the Roman Catholic Church had followed a geometrical trend. Moreover, worldwide missionary expansion has permitted an arithmetical trend too.

or churchgoers. In the case of churchmen, faithfulness was assumed. In fact, it is their ability to accumulate church income that was rewarded. As such, individual economic or spiritual effort was rewarded with capital.

> Monetary pensions from ecclesiastical benefices offered another way to reward faithful servants (Hallman 1985, p. 107).

No theology of Roman Catholic denominations has ever supported capitalistic accumulation. Yet, these theologies have roots grounded in the Original Sin, which have permitted the capitalistic expansion of the Roman Catholic Church. Sin and the need for repentance allowed the Church to collect monies from its flock. In Latin countries, as the sole church, it has operated like a monopoly, enabling perpetual rents from Christians until the Reformation (Davidson and Ekelund Jr. 1997). The summation of which accumulated the monetary capital of the Church, and the reinvestment thereof in lucrative properties contributed to the accumulation process. On the other hand, rewards of faithful servants from church equity acknowledged effort directed at the maximisation of either religious or monetary value.[5] In fact, the leaders of the Roman Catholic Church have historically behaved as capitalistic entrepreneurs and, like other monotheisms, Roman Catholicism has held the spirit of capitalism.

4 Islam, the Arab World and Early Capitalistic Practices

As in Protestantism, Judaism or Catholicism, Islam has evolved alongside capitalism and has integrated its aims and methods (Aqbal and Mirakhor 2006; Gambling and Karim 1991; Iqbal 1997; Rodinson 1966; Taqi-Usmani 2002; Tinker 2004; Zubair 1983). To these authors, there 'is the recognition that there is a basic affinity between the economic scheme of Islam and the capitalistic system' (Zubair 1983, p. 3).

[5] Nowadays, similar rewards from the company's equity are the counterpart of acknowledged effort of performance. Such practices uphold individual accumulation of capital on the basis of the pursuit of the common good. Today incentives utilised in companies seem to play a similar role. In a similar way to how Jewish people held the spirit of capitalism, Catholic theologies have surprisingly led to capitalistic practices.

They unanimously agree that Islam has been seeking for the increase of collective wellbeing. At the collective level, this consists of decreasing poverty and social inequality. For that purpose, Allah rewards collective effort. Islam suggests that every single person shall be rewarded in accordance with his or her merits and efforts. These are understood as comprising actual contributions to the increase of the collective wellbeing. The higher the contribution, the higher the reward. This may result in the main contributors to collective wellbeing accumulating the most capital. Thus the social justice ideal operates as an incentive for the private accumulation of capital.

> Islam, like Capitalism, permits private ownership of property including the means of production and grants freedom of enterprise. It holds trade and therefore production in high esteem. Islam is neither opposed to competitive effort nor is averse to the operation of the market forces.

When doing business, Muslims are to honour the principles of the Sharia, namely the imperative of social justice (Gambling and Karim 1991; Tinker 2004; Zubair 1983). This implies that market forces may not lead to undue earnings at the expense of a Muslim. Undue earnings are regarded as prices disconnected from value. In Islam, the strongest distortion stems from future arrangements. In brief, Islam has developed cash trade. The price is paid when the item is delivered; wages are paid when work is completed. For the same reasons, interest is prohibited, insofar as it enriches the creditor at the expense of the debtor. The creditor accumulates capital, although he is idle. Accordingly, society is morally and socially indebted to him in no way (Rodinson 1966). Wealthier people are responsible for the community. Their wealth must be shared with those in need. In particular, the more capital they accumulate, the higher alms they can pay. These grants will contribute to decreasing social inequalities. Symmetrically, their contribution will increase the collective wellbeing.

Like the Jewish People in Europe, Muslims have developed trade and banking activities in the Middle East since the Low Middle Ages. These activities were what upheld the Meccan Trade (Crone 2004). This relates to the obligation for every Muslim to do a pilgrimage to the Mecca once in their life. For Crone, the Meccan Trade consists of the organisation of the pilgrimage. If some were not able to pay for the pilgrimage, Mecca was allowed to lend them money. The richer paid for themselves and subsidised the poorer pilgrims. The Meccan Trade operates as a trustee that collects money from the rich and distributes to the poor. Here, capitalistic undertakings serve to decrease social inequalities. In brief, Islam has given birth to the spirit of Eastern capitalism.

Conclusion

It is possible to draw three sets of conclusions from the present study. First, capitalistic rationality and double-entry bookkeeping emerged long before the industrial revolution. Accordingly, their spirit has evolved alongside the development of the three monotheisms. The second conclusion appears as a corollary of the former. The spirit of capitalism and double-entry bookkeeping is not the sole possession of Protestantism. The double heuristics of double-entry bookkeeping has consisted of moralising trade relationships and of managing God's blessings. Therefore, the spirit of double-entry bookkeeping has been manifested not in just a single religion but in the three monotheisms. The third conclusion is a delineated from the other two and concerns accounting. There has been a tendency to systematically conflate calculative sciences into financial matters. The religious spirit of accounting evidences that books of accounts can have values other than just monetary ones. Faithful conduct and the soul as working units are not accounted for as monetary items in religious books. Nonetheless, they are central to the evaluation models of faith. In brief, accounting as a spiritual practice upholds self-management. As an economic practice, it upholds the management of what counts, be it financial or not.

The four monotheisms and capitalism have evolved coevally Noticeably, these four religions contribute to the overall spirit of capitalism in different respects. The spirit of industrial and bourgeois capitalism was revealed in the Protestant ethic. It was born in Northern Europe in the nineteenth century and its expansion ended in the late 1960s when financial and international capitalism overcame it (Boltanski and Chiapello 1999,

	Geographic influence	Type of influence	Form of Capitalism
Protestantism	Northern Europe	Theological	Industrial and bourgeois Capitalism
Judaism	Northern Europe	Practical	International and financial Capitalism
Roman Catholicism	Latin Europe	Practical	Estate Capitalism and incentives-based management
Islam	Middle East	Theological	Social entrepreneur Capitalism

Fig. 2.1 Religions and the spirit of Capitalism

2006). Judaism has held the spirit of international and financial capitalism since the Middle Ages. The new spirit of capitalism (international trade and *haute finance*) is very much indebted to the early practices of Judaism. Unexpectedly, the theology of the Original Sin of the Roman Catholic Church has resulted in it engendering estate capitalism and management by incentives in Latin countries. Moreover, the Roman Catholic Church has been the earliest capitalistic organisation until the secularisation of Western societies in the late twentieth century. Finally, Islam has infused the spirit of social capitalism and private entrepreneurship. Altogether, the four religions have shaped the capitalistic sector. The table below summarises these conclusions (Fig. 2.1).

Bibliography

Aho, J. (2005). *Confession and bookkeeping—The religious, moral, and rhetorical roots of modern accounting*. New York: State University of New York Press.

Aqbal, Z., & Mirakhor, A. (2006). *Introduction to Islamic finance: Theory and practice*. London: John Wiley & Sons.

Boltanski, L., & Chiapello, E. (1999). *Le nouvel esprit du Capitalisme*. Paris: La Découverte.

Boltanski, L., & Chiapello, E. (2006). *The new spirit of capitalism*. London: Verso.

Bryer, R. (2000a). The history of accounting and the transition to capitalism in England. Part one: Theory. *Accounting Organizations and Society, 25*(2), 131–162.

Bryer, R. (2000b). The history of accounting and the transition to capitalism in England. Part two: Evidence. *Accounting Organizations and Society, 25*(4–5), 327–381.

Bryer, R. A. (1993). Double-entry bookkeeping and the birth of capitalism: Accounting for the commercial revolution in medieval Northern Italy. *Critical Perspectives on Accounting, 4*(2), 113–140.

Carruthers, B. G., & Espeland, W. N. (1991). Accounting for rationality: Double-entry bookkeeping and the rhetoric of economic rationality. *The American Journal of Sociology, 97*(1), 31–69.

Chiapello, E. (2007). Accounting and the birth of the notion of Capitalism. *Critical Perspectives on Accounting, 18*(3), 263–296.

Crone, P. (2004). *Meccan trade and the rise of Islam*. Princeton, NJ: Princeton University Press.

Davidson, A., & Ekelund Jr., R. (1997). The medieval church and rents from marriage market regulations. *Journal of Economic Behavior and Organization, 32*, 215–245.

Deeg, R. (2009). The rise of internal capitalist diversity? Changing patterns of finance and corporate governance in Europe. *Economy and Society, 38*(4), 552–579.

Derks, H. (2008). Religion, capitalism and the rise of double-entry bookkeeping. *Accounting Business and Financial History, 18*(2), 187–213.

Duby, G. (1979). *Saint Bernard: l'art cistércien*. Paris: Flammarion.

Gambling, T., & Karim, R. A. (1991). *Business and accounting ethics in Islam*. London: Continuum International Publishing.

Hallman, B. (1985). *Italian cardinals, reform and the church as property*. Los Angeles: University of California Press.

Iqbal, Z. (1997). Islamic financial systems. *Finance and Development, 34*(2), 42–45.

Lane, C., & Geoffrey, W. (2009). Capitalist diversity and diversity within capitalism. *Economy and Society, 38*(4), 531–551.

Maltby, J. (1997). Accounting and the soul of the middle-class: Gustav Freytag's *Soll und Haben*. *Accounting Organizations and Society, 22*(1), 69–87.

McKernan, J. F., & Kosmala, K. (2004). Accounting, love and justice. *Accounting Auditing and Accountability Journal, 17*(3), 327–360.

McKernan, J. F., & Kosmala, K. (2007). Doing the truth: Religion—Deconstruction—Justice, and accounting. *Accounting Auditing and Accountability Journal, 20*(5), 729–764.

McPhail, K., & Walters, D. (2009). *Accounting and business ethics—An introduction*. London: Routledge.

Michaud, C. (1991). *L'Eglise et l'argent sous l'Ancien Régime—Les receveurs généraux du clergé de France aux XVIè—XVIIIè siècles*. Paris: Fayard.

Miller, P., & Napier, C. (1993). Genealogies of calculation. *Accounting Organizations and Society, 18*(7–8), 631–647.

Quattrone, P. (2009). Books to be practiced: Memory, the power of the visual, and the success of accounting. *Accounting, Organizations and Society, 34*(1), 85–118.

Rodinson, M. (1966). *Islam and capitalism*. London: Saqi Essentials.

Sombart, W. (1911). *The Jews and modern capitalism*. Kitchener, ON: Batoche Books Limited.

Taqi-Usmani, M. (2002). *An introduction to Islamic finance (Arab and Islamic laws)*. Boston, MA: CQ Press.

Tinker, A. M. (2004). The enlightenment and its discontents: Antinomies of Christianity, Islam and the calculative sciences. *Accounting Auditing and Accountability Journal, 17*(3), 442–475.

Weber, M. (1921). *The Protestant ethic and the spirit of capitalism*. New York: Routledge.

Weber, M. (1922). *Economy and society*. Berkeley, CA: The University of California Press.

Zubair, H. (1983). Theory of profit: The Islamic viewpoint. *Journal of Research on Islamic Economics, 1*(1), 3–14.

3

The Book as the Spirits of Accounting

This chapter extends the Chap. 2 by showing how each of the book's four religions defines and constructs an accounting spirituality, thereby encouraging believers to keep metaphoric accounts of their faithful conduct. Judaism encourages believers to account for duties ordered by God. Roman Catholicism has developed a system of accounting for souls, sacraments and sins as well as having the first international reporting standards. In Islam, the believer is to account for the Sharia. Lastly, in Protestantism, the believer accounts for all blessings received from God and all paybacks for those blessings.

As highlighted in this book's introduction, accounting's birth is coincidental to that of the book's studied religions. As the economic and accounting literature tends to agree that giving an account is coincidental to the birth of capitalism, it seems that accounting and religion emerged alongside each other. Although such a syllogism could be critiqued, it is very useful to understand how the book has enabled the rise of a spirituality deeply grounded in what is now known as double-entry bookkeeping.

This chapter delineates each of the four main monotheisms' spiritualities leading to metaphorical balanced accounts of faith. Under this purview, and following Weber (1922) as well as Sombart (1911), accounting vocabulary is adapted to a religious context's peculiarities. As credits are what is received, they are termed *From God*. On the other hand, debits are what is owed or given back and are therefore called

V. Joannidès de Lautour, *Accounting, Capitalism and the Revealed Religions*, DOI 10.1007/978-3-319-32333-6_3

To God. Using this religious terminology instead of the usual debits and credits allows to depart from mere economic transactions and systematic monetary evaluation. So doing enables the revealing of accounting's core concern and issue, as a practice which consists of ensuring communion between mankind and God.[1]

Grounded in the history of religious thought, this chapter shows how each religion's authorities developed a specific accounting theology and spirituality. A very similar timeframe is understood for the four, as in the Middle Ages where the bitterness of religious disputes was aimed at making the identity of each religion unique. Thence, this chapter follows the chronology of theological disputes: Judaism, Roman Catholicism, Islam and Protestantism.

1 Accounting for the Law in Judaism

In the rabbinic literature, most authors agree that common understandings relate to God's identity, revelation and commandments. After millennia of paganism, God revealed the Tablets to Moses on Mount Sinai. All commentators agree that the core commandment guiding the understanding of God's identity, capabilities and will is the honouring of His uniqueness—idolatry being the main offense against God, Who was not to be personified through any icons (Copeland 2002; Kaplan 1998; Neusner 1993; Ross 1999; Schechter 1894a, b; Ward 1999). Subsequently, no representation of the Lord was allowed. At the same time as the Lord gave Moses the Tablets, He revealed to His people His law and counterparts through a covenant (Urbach 1979). The people of Israel were to honour Him and were in turn rewarded or punished in this life as well as in the next (Neusner 1979, 1993; Schechter 1895b, 1896; Urbach 1979). Such common understandings have been driven by the consciousness of being chosen by God to reveal Him to the world. The rabbinic belief in the election of Israel finds its clearest expression in a prayer commencing as follows (see Schechter 1894b):

[1] Some argue that accounting seeks to reconcile good and evil, assuming a moral role played by book records.

> Thou hast chosen from all peoples; thou hast loved and taken pleasure in us, and hast exalted above all tongues; thou hast sanctified by thy commandments and brought near unto thy service; O this King, thou hast called by thy great and holy name.

Eventually, Moses was chosen by God to free the people of Israel from Egyptian enslavement. Since its Exodus from Egypt, the Jewish people have been considered His witnesses worldwide, saved by God (Elman 1994; Satlow 2003). After Moses died, a Messiah had been expected, whose coming was to reflect ultimate salvation. It is commonly understood that honouring God's Law expressed through the Ten Commandments and the Sabbath collectively and individually is the sole path to salvation (Elman 1994; Jaffee 1997; Lévinas and Aronowicz 1990; Satlow 2003; Schechter 1895a, b, 1896).[2]

> The faith that the Messiah will restore the Kingdom of Israel, which under his sceptre will extend over the whole world. 2. The notion that a last terrible battle will take place with the enemies of God (or of Israel), who will strive against the establishment of the kingdom, and who will finally be destroyed. 3. The conviction that it will be an age of both material as well as spiritual happiness for all those who are included in the kingdom (Schechter 1895a, p. 206).

Obviously, these have been the foundations of the Jewish Law and rules for everyday life.[3] Initially, rules were 613 in number and covered all aspects of life, 365 being prohibitive laws (and as many sanctions), whereas the other 248 were affirmative and accounted for (Urbach 1996). The rabbinic literature, such as synthesised by Urbach (1996), explains that

[2] See Exodus 27: 2 and Leviticus 18: 2.

[3] The Old Testament (viz. the Jewish Bible) evokes on numerous occasions that the believer must account for his conduct and for God's gifts (see in Genesis 1: 22–28, 3: 16, 6: 1, 8: 17, 9: 1–7, 16: 10, 17: 2–20, 22: 17, 26: 4–24, 28: 3, 35: 11, 48: 4; Exodus: 1: 10, 7: 3, 23: 29, 32: 13; Leviticus 26: 9; Deuteronomy 6: 3, 7: 13, 8: 1–13, 13: 17, 30: 16; Leviticus 7: 12–16, 22: 29; I Chronicles 4: 27; Job 19: 18; Psalms 16: 4, 107: 38; Proverbs 6: 35; Isaiah 51: 2; Jeremiah 23: 3, 29: 6, 30: 19, 33: 22; Ezekiel 36: 10–11, 37: 26; Hosea 4: 10, 12: 1; Amos 4: 4; Nahum 3: 15; Chronicles 11: 11, 16: 19; Esther 10: 2; Prophets: Isaiah 2: 22; Ezekiel 12: 19, 16: 61, 24: 13; Nehemiah 12: 8–46; Daniel 6: 2; Amos 4: 5, 8: 8; Jonah 1: 7–8, 2–9; Psalm 26: 7, 50: 14–23, 100: 4, 107: 22, 116: 17, 147: 7; Jeremiah 30: 19).

every day brings its new temptation to be resisted only by a strict *Do-Not*. On the other hand, the whole man stands in the service of God, each part of his body being entrusted with the execution of its respective functions (Urbach 1996, pp. 355–361). Then, David came and reduced these commandments to eleven, Isaiah to six, Micah to three, Isaiah to two and lastly Amos and Habakkuk to one: 'seek the Lord and live by faith'. Ultimately, the school of Elijah Tanna exclaims: 'Let man fulfil the commandments of the Torah with joy and then they will be *counted to him* as righteousness' (emphasis added), which opens to accounting records and procedures as routines in Jewish thought (Cohen 1936; Schechter 1896; Sombart 1911; Urbach 1979).

Judaism has suggested that believers should practice metaphoric books of accounts, in which faith in God is recorded as *From God* and should be balanced through actual conduct reflecting mankind's indebtedness *To God* (Sombart 1911). Actual conduct and required duties performed were expected to match. As rabbinic literature states, the believer is bound to God through a direct relationship resulting in him or her identifying individually what the Lord expects. In Jewish theologies, faith offered by God should lead the believer to conduct him or herself righteously (that is, consistently with His expectations).

> Whether one is accounted 'righteous' or 'wicked' depends on the balance of commands performed and commands neglected. Obviously this necessitates the keeping of accounts, and each man therefore has his own, in which his words and his deeds, even the words spoken in jest, are all carefully registered. According to one authority (*Ruth Rabba, 33a*) the prophet Elijah keeps these accounts, according to another (*Esther Rabba, 86a*) the duty is assigned to angels. Every man has thus an account in heaven: Israel has a particularly large one (*Sifra, 446*). And one of the ways of preparing for death is to have this account ready [...] It is not difficult to perceive that the keeping of these accounts was no easy matter (Sombart 1911, pp. 146–147).

Effectively, 'man is rewarded for duties performed and punished for duties neglected, the rewards and punishments being received partly in this world and partly in the next world' (Sombart 1911, p. 144). Such religious accounts are underpinned by the fact that the God of the prophets is a responsive God making moral demands that humans are free to obey or disobey. The Lord also reacts to human actions in judgement through rewards and retributions (Ward 1999, p. 164). The believer records his or her life on a daily basis and keeps these records secret ready for Judgement Day. A twofold relationship to God is revealed through these books of accounts. Firstly, in this life, the believer is rewarded when commanded duties are completed; the individual is in peace and acknowledged by other community members as a righteous person (Urbach 1979, p. 380). Conversely, if duties are not performed, man is punished on earth through public revelation of guilty conduct and the absence of peace (Urbach 1979, p. 373).

In addition to such counterparts, on Judgement Day the individual encounters God. The regularity and contents of the accounts is verified by the Lord. If accounts are not fair in terms of the actual conduct of life, the self will be punished in the next life. God is omniscient and cannot be cheated: He can easily identify such fairness. If accounts are fair, reward becomes possible but is enabled only if *From God* and *To God* records are balanced. Balance or imbalance is appraised and compared on the basis of biographic accounts of commandments and performance. In case of imbalance, the believer may sincerely repent him or herself and is rewarded for acknowledging poor conduct and being fair going forwards (Urbach 1979, p. 466). The rabbinic literature insists on the privacy of such books and the prohibition of any intrusion between God and the believer (Cohen 1936), as nobody can know the value of a commandment but the Lord in person (Costa 2004).

Faith is given by God and is recorded as *From God*. By faith, the believer must fulfil duties ordered by the Lord and accounts for them as *To God*. Fulfilled duties balance commandments from faith. A balanced book is rewarded by the Lord, rewards being the net result and therefore accounted for as *From God* (Urbach 1979, p. 466; Sombart 1911, p. 144). As unfulfilled duties are missing, faith has no counterpart. These are first recorded as an offence to God, diminishing value to Him, namely as negative *To God* (wicked conduct) and are compensated through retributions *From God*. Retributions are expected in this life, for the offender to have a chance to rebalance the account. If missing duties are not performed at all, upon death the Jewish person is punished in the afterlife. The figure below summarises the contents of these biographic accounts (Fig. 3.1).

To God	From God
Performed duties	Faith in God
(Unfulfilled obligations)	Retributions and rewards in this life
	Retributions and rewards in the next life

Fig. 3.1 Accounting for the law in Judaism

2 Accounting for Original Sin in Roman Catholicism

In Christian theologies, it is commonplace to consider God revealed to the world through Trinity: the Father, Jesus and the Holy Spirit. In Aquinas' theology, God is beyond essence and understanding. This requires mediation between Him and the self (Torrell 2002), this need for mediation being accentuated by the theology of the Original Sin: Adam and Eve ate the apple from the knowledge tree and thereby expected to know and equal God.[4] Therefore, Christian theologies agree that clergy is the sole group qualified to approach God and should intercede between Him and believers. The very first intermediary was Jesus, sent to clean mankind's sins (Cohen 1980; Harrison 2002; Norman 1997; Torrell 2002).

The sinning nature of mankind leads Catholic theologians to consider that divine grace and salvation are not acquired: people are justified by their acts, believers having to work for it. That is, evil leads to Hell (Dante 1314), good work to Paradise (Dante 1321) and repentance for poor conduct to Purgatory before God decides to send the guilty to Hell or Paradise (Dante 1316). Moreover, Jansenist theologians consider that divine grace is not granted to all, God selecting amongst men those who shall be saved (Pascal 1656). As nobody knows who will be saved, demonstrations of faith through acts should be made: people bet that they might be saved.

[4] See Genesis 3: 1–13.

At best, they are saved; at worst, they go to Purgatory in lieu of Hell (Pascal 1670). Considered sinners in nature, believers are expected to be justified through confession of sins and subsequent repentance (Saint Augustin 1637).

Rules driving justification were based on the notion of a path to God (Pascal 1670) consisting of seven sacraments, each of them characterising a stage in Christian life (Case 1907; Christie 1918; Panofsky 1951). Eventually, seven days after birth, children were to be baptised, baptism meaning entry into God's community. Seven years later, by the age of reason, communion was received, whereby the child accepts God as Lord and Jesus Christ as saviour. Seven years later, as teenagers, they receive confirmation, whereby they repeat the prior oath. When they become adults, marriage is celebrated by a priest or a deacon. Some receive ordination as the fifth sacrament. Ultimately, shortly before passing away, last rites are received. Throughout their entire life, believers receive Eucharist in the course of the service, whereby they iterate faith in their Saviour and Lord weekly. To be allowed to receive Eucharist, believers were to confess their sins (Saint-Augustin 1637).[5] Since the High Middle Ages confessional bookkeeping has dominated Catholic spirituality (Aho 2005). As such, each person was accounted for as a soul, each of which was to have some of the sacraments as a counterpart (Hoskin and Macve 1986; Quattrone 2004, 2009).

Although medievalists have traditionally acknowledged that the Roman Catholic Church has accounted for the Original Sin through sacramental and confessional accounting, they have remained elusive regarding procedures adopted (Aho 2005; Joannidès 2011). However, accounting scholars have focused on records in the books practiced by the Catholic Church acting on behalf of the Lord (Aho 2005; Hoskin and Macve 1986; Quattrone 2004, 2009).

> Each person's credits and debits [...] are entered not just once, but twice: first in the Book of Accounts, a judicial record kept on earth by humanity, and again in the Book of Life, a register of citizenship in [heaven] (Aho 2005, p. xv).

[5] See Leviticus 16: 21, 26: 40; Numbers 5: 7; Psalms 32: 5, 38: 18; John 9: 22, 12: 42; Acts 24: 14; Romans 10: 9, 14: 11; Philippians 2: 11; I Timothy 3: 16; James 5: 16; I John 1: 9, 4: 3; II John 1: 7; Revelation of John 3: 5, 11: 1–13.

Absence of a counterpart in the book of accounts was considered a sin, while the account of life was unbalanced (Aho 2005). Rebalancing it through indulgences sold by God's representatives, that is clergy members (Quattrone 2004), was mandatory. If the account happened to be unbalanced, the believer was to do penance. In the first instance, the guilty person was to say a given amount of prayers or to pay a fine for evil conduct to rebalance the account. In the second book of accounts, sins were recorded. Again, an indulgence expressed in monetary terms corresponded to a sin (Quattrone 2004). In practice, the believer self-accounted for one's conduct on a daily basis and submitted his or her biographical records to the priest—they being the sole person capable of appraising them and saying whether they might be pardoned. As sins were viewed as destroyers of God's creation, they were accounted for as negative values in *To God* records. Subsequently, rebalancing the account required indulgences to be greater than sins and paid on penance time (Aho 2005). The keeping of such personal accounts followed clerical procedures and language.

> Penance is required of all believers beyond the Ages of discretion at least once a year, preferably more often. This, with a priest [...] It consists of three parts: contrition, confession proper, and satisfaction [...] After rehearsing their case, penitents must approach the sitting priest and in the sight of all—the private booth would come later—clearly, frankly and humbly disclose their sins; not, it must be emphasized, their 'sins in general only', but 'one by one', according to their species and number, situating each in the circumstances that occasioned it (Aho 2005, pp. 19–20).

The priest appraised compliance of conduct with the church laws and the regularity of accounting records. The sole appraisal of churchgoers' behaviour, balanced accounts and subsequent rewards (booking a seat in Heaven) or punishments (promise of Purgatory or Hell) were means of maintaining the sacred sanctuary. Effectively, the universalistic and holistic heuristic of the Roman Catholic Church required homogeneous records and application of the doctrine worldwide. Therefore, the Holy See issued standards for the recording of souls, sins and sacraments: souls were accounted for as given *From God*, whereas *To God* records encompassed the seven sacraments (Aho 2005), as well as sins and corresponding indulgences (Aho 2005; Hoskin and Macve 1986; Quattrone 2004, 2009). As sins were an offence against the soul offered by God, they were accounted for as negative, which required rebalance through subsequent indulgence. In territories, cardinals were to enforce the accounting system, whereas bishops in dioceses were to compel priests and congregations to everyday application (Hallman 1985). All congregations were to record the same books and report them to the upper hierarchical level for approbation. The figure below summarises biographic accounts in Counter-Reformation Roman Catholicism (Fig. 3.2).

To God	From God
Books of life	**Soul**
7 sacraments	
Baptism	
Communion	
Confirmation	
Marriage	
Ordination	
Eucharist	
Last rites	
Indulgence (if imbalance)	
Books of account	
(Sin)	
Indulgence	

Fig. 3.2 Accounting for the holy sacraments in Roman Catholicism

3 Accounting for the Sharia in Islam

Historically, Islam appeared later than Judaism and Christianity and has been considered to have borrowed from both religions. Common understandings of Allah are similar to those of the Christians' God, that is the almighty Creator punishing unfaithful people forever or promising Paradise for the just. Allah is commonly presented as the incarnation of Justice (Rodinson 1966). As the Eternal in Judaism, Allah was revealed to the Prophet through Angel Gabriel to whom He gave instructions regarding the conduct of a holy and just life. During his life, the Prophet was the Lord's messenger on earth and delivered the Sharia. In Islam, Jesus Christ is an apostle of God and not His son, which does not prevent believers from awaiting his return (Décobert 2004; Murata and Chittik 1994; Tapper and Tapper 1987).

When the believer passes away, he or she stands trial before Allah, Who appraises the consistency of conduct with the Sharia. Remarkably, judgement day in Islam is called the 'Day of Accounts', on which the deceased person introduces to the Lord the biographic accounts he or she has kept. If accounts are consistent with prescriptions from the Sharia, the person will be declared just and sent to Paradise. On the contrary, if the person is declared unjust, as retribution in the next life they will be sent to Hell. However, as in Jansenist theology, Islam is characterised by predestination, God selecting ex ante those who shall be saved, others being left to conduct themselves as if they were chosen. At worst, they will not be rewarded, while at best Paradise is promised. Again, the Pascalian bet, prevailing in Jansenist theology, can apply to Islam (Mohammed 2000; Thomson 1950a, b; Watt 1946).

Rules enforced to arrive at Salvation rest upon the honoured of the Sharia, namely Islam's five pillars: faith in the Oneness of God and the finality of the prophethood of Muhammad,[6] establishment of the daily prayers, concern for and almsgiving to the needy, self-purification through fasting, and pilgrimage to Mecca for those who can (Murata and Chittik 1994; Rodinson 1966). Eventually, the Sharia operates as the Law in Judaism, the five pillars being similar to the duties ordered by God (Torrey 1967). It also acts as sacramental accounting in Christianity,

[6] Hereby, I do not address theological debates regarding prophet identity leading to dichotomies between Shiaism and Sunnism. I do not question here whether the right Prophet in Islam is Muhammad or Ali.

as daily prayers, casual almsgiving, annual fasting (on Ramadan) and pilgrimage to Mecca are recorded as events driving life (Rodinson 1966).

Routines developed borrow from earlier monotheisms and rely on recording in books all events of life. In Islamic literature, every believer is supervised by two angels keeping biographic books of accounts. The angel on the right of the believer records his or her good actions, while the other on his or her left records all bad actions. Once merged, these accounts summarise how the faithful believer honoured the five pillars of Islam. Thence, their honouring is recorded as *To God* balancing faith (Rodinson 1966; Torrey 1967). In case of imbalance between commandments and actual conduct, retributions are expected in the next life (Hell), which reads as follows (Fig. 3.3):

As salvation can be obtained through acts, the angel must record other daily events and their impact on Allah's Creations (Gambling and Karim 1991; Murata and Chittik 1994; Rodinson 1966). In particular, actions directed at increasing the wellbeing of Allah's people must be accounted for. At the collective level, this consists of decreasing poverty and social inequality, for which purpose collective effort is rewarded. At all times, the believer must seek for the counterpart of his or her conduct: beneficiary or casualty. If conduct increases others' wellbeing, it is rewarded.

To God	From God
Islam's five pillars Praising one God and His Prophet Establishment of daily prayers Concern for and almsgiving to the needy Self-purification through fasting Pilgrimage to Mecca	Faith in God Retributions and rewards in the next life

Fig. 3.3 Account of life for the Sharia in Islam

On the contrary, if it decreases one piece of Creation, reparation is required. A common example is that of accidental death: if a believer accidentally kills another person, he or she is indebted to the victim's family unto death and must repair in accordance with his or her capabilities (Murata and Chittik 1994; Rodinson 1966; Smith 1957; Torrey 1967).[7]

Every feature of each Islamic person's life was recorded in the Book of Accounts; so were counterparts. When a Muslim held money, the counterpart appeared in the book. If a transaction happened to spoil a counterpart, the guilty person was prosecuted: unfair and dishonest conduct was punished. In particular, Islamic bookkeeping has pointed out how believers honour the ideal of social justice as well as the prohibition of interest and speculation.[8] The following recitations from the Quran instance this:

> But this Lord is Most forgiving, full of Mercy. If He were to call them (at once) to account for what they have earned, then surely He would have hastened their punishment: but they have their appointed time, beyond which they will find no refuge (Al-Kahf 18: 58).
>
> Verily I shall give life to the dead, and I record that which they send before and that which they leave behind, and of all things have I taken account in a clear Book [of evidence] (Yaa Seen 36: 12).[9]

In both recitations, Islamic faithfulness rests upon an accounting system in which conduct is accounted for twice. The goods that the self left behind are accounted for as *From God.* The goods sent to Heaven are accounted for as *To God.* One could summarise Islamic accounting spirituality as the recording of good and evil actions and their counterparts, in other words beneficiaries or casualties. Muslims introduce their book to Allah Who rewards good

[7] The same principle applies to business and other economic transactions. As stated in the methodology section, these are beyond the scope of this study and are accordingly not developed in this book.

[8] Nowadays, Islamic finance and bookkeeping translate principled prohibition of interest and of speculative conduct and rest upon the notion of property rights, risk sharing, sanctity of contracts and Sharia-approved activities.

[9] For further insights into revealed accounting procedures, see Al Baqarah 2: 225, 2: 233, 2: 284; Ale'Imraan 3: 11, 3: 62, 3: 199; An-Nisaa' 4: 86; Al-Maa'idah 5: 89; Al-An'aam 6: 34, 6: 44, 6: 52; Al-'Araaf 7: 95; An-Nahl 16: 46, 16: 47, 16: 56, 16: 93; Maryam 19: 94; An-Noor 24: 39; Ash-Shu'araa' 26: 113; Al-Qasas 28: 78; Al-Ankaboot 29: 13; As-Saafaat37: 18; Saad 38: 16, 38: 26, 38: 39, 38: 53; Ghaafir 40: 21, 40: 22, 40: 27; Ash-Shooraa 42: 22; Az-Zukhruf 43: 18; Al-Fath 48: 25; Qaaf 50: 4; Adh-Dhaariyaat 51: 60; Al-Haaqah 69: 20, 69: 26; Al-Jinn 72: 13, 72: 28; Al-Inshiqaq 84: 8.

To God	From God
Conduct Compensation	Beneficiaries/Casualties (as God's creatures affected)

Fig. 3.4 Account of transactions for the Sharia in Islam

conduct and punishes evil actions. The double-entry design of the book sheds light on the nature of the honouring of Islamic principles (Fig. 3.4).

To ensure that believers would conform to the principles of the Sharia in their day-to-day conduct, Arab mathematicians might have first intuited double-entry bookkeeping (Aho 2005). The invention of the so-called Arab numbers allowed the birth of modern arithmetic and calculation, which Roman numbers did not enable. This inspired Luca Paccioli's theory of double-entry bookkeeping. Although Tinker (2001) refutes the idea that modern accounting is a direct discovery of Islam, as the majority of Muslims were not acquainted with these scientific discoveries, most scholars consider accounting to have been an indirect discovery of Islam (Crone 2004; Gambling and Karim 1991; Iqbal 1997; Iqbal and Mirakhor 2006; Napier 2009; Taqi-Usmani 2002; Tinker 2004; Zubair 1983).

4 Accounting for Blessings in Protestantism

In a study on the religious affiliation of German industry leaders, Weber (1921) observed that these tended to be Protestants rather than Catholics. He ascribed this situation to the Protestant ethic, which encourages capitalistic undertaking and success. On the contrary, money and capital are taboos within Roman Catholicism. To meet God's requirements, the individual must respond to His calling, which consists of vocational work (*Beruf*: calling, vocation, profession). If the individual works well, God rewards him through the compensation that he receives. The greater this is, the more pleasing you are to God. The connection to Divine Grace appears later (p. 125), when Weber stresses that the self only must seek to know what God decided and to preserve that confidence in Jesus Christ that results from actual faith. Protestantism suggests believers counting God's blessings and thanking Him for those (Weber 1921).[10] In the same way do they account for maledictions. The following is the refrain of a traditional Protestant canticle.

Count your blessings, name them one by one,
Count your blessings, see what God hath done!
Count your blessings, name them one by one,
And it will surprise you what the Lord hath done.

For Weber, the most obvious blessing is capitalistic success in particular and succeeding at undertakings in general. If successful, any undertaking has been validated and blessed by God Himself. The notion of thankfulness for those results in believers counting their thankful praises.[11] They have two books of accounts. It is expected that both accounts should be balanced. The consolidation of the two sets of records results in double-entry books. God's blessings are gifts entrusted by God and are recorded as for credit. Symmetrically, thankful conduct is their counterpart and is accounted for as debit. Credit is given a priori; the believer constructs the debit records accordingly so that debit balances credit.

Weber specifies the content of the debits. These consist of praising and praying. Periodically, the Protestant utilises prayer as the very device for communicating with God (Lévinas 1975). When praying, he thanks Him for His blessings and acknowledges His magnificence. Thereby, he acknowledges the Lord's almightiness. In brief, the Protestant praises Him. Thankful conduct consists of utilising God's blessings wisely. To this end, the believer records in a book what shall be the outcomes of his

[10] The following paragraphs summarise *The Protestant Ethic and the Spirit of Capitalism*. As the book is supposedly well-known, I deliberately do not quote Weber literally.

[11] For Biblical insights into accountability for God's blessings, see in the New Testament Matthew 5: 11, 12: 36, 13: 21; Mark 4: 17; Luke 1: 3, 6: 22, 16: 2, 9: 23, 19: 3; John 12: 9–11, 14: 11, 15: 21; in the Epistles: Romans 14: 12; I Corinthians 14: 24; II Corinthians 10: 10; Philippians 1: 24; Colossians 3: 6, 4: 3; Philemon 1: 18; Hebrews 4: 13, 13: 17; I Peter 4: 5. These references are to be supplemented with those of footnote 5. Indeed, references from the Old Testament apply to Protestantism too.

faithful conduct. He self-records how he plans to use his gifts as well as what he expects from them. Only afterwards, he can compare his actuality with the expectations. Thanks to such dashboards, he can measure the performance of his own conduct and the extent to which he honours God. By his conduct, the believer is called to direct his capabilities and skills at the maximisation of capitalistic profit. In order to be pleasing to God, the Protestant shall use his gifts in the most efficient and rational way. Thirdly, thankful conduct consists of paying back for God's blessings. The individual self-evaluates the amount to be paid. He then can refund his congregation accordingly.

In the three cases, Protestants rely on their own judgement. Nobody knows better than they do for what to thank God. In the same vein, nobody is able to tell how to thank and how much to refund. It is the believer who evaluates these on his own. Analogously, he self-appraises what wise use of God's gifts would mean. It is his responsibility that he erects a comprehensive rational evaluation system. It is his responsibility too that he always relies on that model for appraising the counterparts of God's blessings. As faith is the very intimacy of the individual (Lévinas 1975), the same blessing can be accounted for differently from one person to another (McKernan and Kosmala 2007). Such Protestant views on accounting seem to stem from the fact that Protestantism is the modern form of early Judaism (Sombart 1916) (Fig. 3.5).

To God	**From God**
Repayments **Prayer and Praise** **Volunteering** **Witness** **Donations**	**Blessings** **Soul** **Salvation** **Divine Grace**

Fig. 3.5 Account of blessings in Protestantism

Bibliography

Aho, J. (2005). *Confession and bookkeeping—The religious, moral, and rhetorical roots of modern accounting*. New York: State University of New York Press.

Case, S. (1907). Authority for the sacraments. *The BIblical World, 29*(5), 357–360.

Christie, F. (1918). Church and sacraments. *The American Journal of Theology, 22*(1), 143–145.

Cohen, B. (1936). The classifcation of the law in the Mishneh Torah. *The Jewish Quarterly Review, 25*(4), 519–540.

Cohen, J. (1980). Original Sin and the evil inclination: A polemicit's appreciation of human nature. *The Harvard Theological Review, 73*(3/4), 495–520.

Copeland, S. (2002). That law which calls us away from mystifying rapture to religious responsibility. *Journal of Law and Religion, 17*(1/2), 111–119.

Costa, J. (2004). *L'au-delà et la résurrection dans la littérature rabbinique ancienne*. Paris, Louvain: Peeters.

Crone, P. (2004). *Meccan trade and the rise of Islam*. Princeton, NJ: Princeton University Press.

Dante. (1314). *L'Enfer*. Paris: Garnier-Flammarion.

Dante. (1316). *Le Purgatoire*. Paris: Garnier-Flammarion.

Dante. (1321). *Le Paradis*. Paris: Garnier-Flammarion.

Décobert, C. (2004). L'autorité religieuse aux premiers siècles de l'Islam. *Archives des Sciences Sociales des Religions, 125*, 23–44.

Elman, Y. (1994). Argument for the sake of heaven: "The mind of the Talmud". *The Jewish Quarterly Review, 84*(2/3), 261–282.

Gambling, T., & Karim, R. A. (1991). *Business and accounting ethics in Islam*. London: Continuum International Publishing.

Hallman, B. (1985). *Italian cardinals, reform and the church as property*. Los Angeles: University of California Press.

Harrison, P. (2002). Original Sin and the problem of knowledge in early modern Europe. *Journal of History of Ideas, 63*(2), 239–259.

Hoskin, K. W., & Macve, R. H. (1986). Accounting and the examination: A genealogy of disciplinary power. *Accounting Organizations and Society, 11*(2), 105–136.

Iqbal, Z. (1997). Islamic financial systems. *Finance and Development, 34*(2), 42–45.

Iqbal, Z., & Mirakhor, A. (2006). *Introduction to Islamic finance: Theory and practice*. London: John Wiley & Sons.

Jaffee, M. (1997). A Rabbinic ontology of the written and spoken word: On discipleship, transformative knowledge, and the living texts of oral Torah. *Journal of the American Academy of Religion, 65*(3), 525–549.

Joannidès, V. (2011). Du jugement dernier à l'organisation des marchés financiers: une petite histoire de la comptabilité. In FNEGE (Ed.), *Les paradoxes de la gestion des entreprises—entre individualisme et holisme*. Paris: Vuibert.

Kaplan, L. (1998). Israel under the moundain: Emmanuel Levinas on freedom and constraint in the revelation of the Torah. *Modern Judaism, 18*(1), 35–46.

Lévinas, E. (1975). *God, death and time*. Stanford, CA: Stanford Univeristy Press.

Lévinas, E., & Aronowicz, A. (1990). *Nine Talmudic readings*. Bloomington, IL: Indiana University Press.

McKernan, J. F., & Kosmala, K. (2007). Doing the truth: Religion—Deconstruction—Justice, and accounting. *Accounting Auditing and Accountability Journal, 20*(5), 729–764.

Mohammed, I. (2000). Concept of predestination in Islam and Christianity: Special reference to Averroes and Aquinas. *The Islamic Quarterly, 44*(2), 393–413.

Murata, S., & Chittik, W. (1994). *The vision of Islam*. New York: Paragon House.

Napier, C. (2009). Defining Islamic accounting: Current issues, past root. *Accounting History, 14*(1/2), 121–144.

Neusner, J. (1979). *The way of Torah—An introduction to Judaism*. Belmont, CA: Wadsworth Inc..

Neusner, J. (1993). The Mishna in philosophical context and out of canonical bounds. *Journal of Biblical Literature, 112*(2), 291–304.

Norman, A. (1997). Regress and the doctrine of epistemic Original Sin. *The Philosophical Quarterly, 14*(189), 477–494.

Panofsky, E. (1951). Two roger problems: The donor of the hague lamentation and the date of the altarpiece of the seven sacraments. *The Art Bulletin, 33*(1), 33–40.

Pascal, B. (1656). Ecrits sur la grâce. In B. Pascal (Ed.), *De l'esprit géométrique* (pp. 120–140). Paris: Garnier-Flammarion.

Pascal, B. (1670). *Pensées*. Paris: Garnier-Flammarion.

Quattrone, P. (2004). Accounting for god: Accounting and accountability practices in the society of Jesus (Italy, XVI-XVII centuries). *Accounting Organizations and Society, 29*(7), 647–683.

Quattrone, P. (2009). Books to be practiced: Memory, the power of the visual, and the success of accounting. *Accounting Organizations and Society, 34*(1), 85–118.

Rodinson, M. (1966). *Islam and Capitalism*. London: Saqi Essentials.
Ross, J. (1999). The primacy of the personalist concept of god in Jewish thought. *The Journal of Jewish Thought and Philosophy, 8*, 171–199.
Saint-Augustin. (1637). *Les confessions*. Paris: Garnier-Flammarion.
Satlow, M. (2003). And on the earth you shall sleep: *Talmud Torah* and rabbinic ascetism. *The Journal of Religion, 83*(2), 204–225.
Schechter, S. (1894a). Some aspects of rabbinic theology I. *The Jewish Quarterly Review, 6*(3), 405–427.
Schechter, S. (1894b). Some aspects of rabbinic theology II. *The Jewish Quarterly Review, 6*(4), 633–647.
Schechter, S. (1895a). Some aspects of rabbinic theology III. *The Jewish Quarterly Review, 7*(2), 195–215.
Schechter, S. (1895b). Some aspects of rabbinic theology: The "law". *The Jewish Quarterly Review, 8*(1), 1–16.
Schechter, S. (1896). Some aspects of rabbinic theology VI. The Torah in its aspects of law. *The Jewish Quarterly Review, 8*(3), 363–380.
Smith, W. C. (1957). *Islam in modern history*. New York: New American Library.
Sombart, W. (1911). *The Jews and modern Capitalism*. Kitchener, ON: Batoche Books Limited.
Sombart, W. (1916). *Der Moderne Kapitalismus*. München, Leipzig: Duncker und Humbolt.
Tapper, N., & Tapper, R. (1987). The birth of the Prophet: Ritual and gender in Turkish Islam. *Man New Series, 22*(1), 69–92.
Taqi-Usmani, M. (2002). *An introduction to Islamic finance (Arab and Islamic laws)*. Boston, MA: CQ Press.
Thomson, W. (1950a). Free will and predestination in early Islam I. *The Muslim World, 40*(3), 207–216.
Thomson, W. (1950b). Free will and predestination in early Islam II. *The Muslim World, 40*(4), 276–287.
Tinker, A.M. (2001). Paper prohets: an autocritique, *The British Accounting Review, 33*(1), 77–89.
Tinker, A. M. (2004). The enlightenment and its discontents: Antinomies of Christianity, Islam and the calculative sciences. *Accounting Auditing and Accountability Journal, 17*(3), 442–475.
Torrell, J.-P. (2002). *Initiation à Saint Thomas d'Aquin*. Paris: Cerf.
Torrey, C. (1967). *The Jewish foundation of Islam*. Ktav Publishing Inc.
Urbach, E. (1979). *The sages, their beliefs and concepts*. Jerusalem: The Magnes Press, The Hebrew University.

Urbach, E. (1996). *Les sages d'Israël—Conceptions et croyances des maîtres du Talmud*. Verdier: Cerf.

Ward, K. (1999). The god of philosophers and the god of Abraham, Isaac and Jacob. *The Journal of Jewish Thought and Philosophy, 8*, 157–170.

Watt, W. M. (1946). Free will and predestination in early Islam. *The Muslim World, 36*(2), 124–152.

Weber, M. (1921). *The Protestant ethic and the spirit of Capitalism*. New York: Routledge.

Weber, M. (1922). *Economy and Society*. San Francisco, CA: The University of California Press.

Zubair, H. (1983). Theory of profit: The Islamic viewpoint. *Journal of Research on Islamic Economics, 1*(1), 3–14.

4

Religions and Contemporary Accounting Issues

This chapter exposes the lessons that can be drawn from Chap. 3 on the joint development of the book's four religions and double-entry book-keeping. Pursuant of this objective, the Chapter draws lessons pertaining to accounting. Those mostly relate to the evaluation of counterparts, with a particular emphasis placed on intangibles (faith). Also, the four religions initiated a discussion as to the need for reporting and auditing standards. Building on the philosophy of religions, this chapter next discusses how contemporary accountability systems have been influenced by the book's religions.

This chapter discusses the main lessons that can be learnt from the Middle Ages' theological disputes and what their impact on contemporary accounting is. Interestingly, each religion highlights a different dimension of accounting. Whilst it is always very tempting to highlight differences across contexts, ascribing those to 'culture', what is more important is to consider what is common to all of them. So doing means that each context is studied separately, hence it can be analysed down to its core. A very good way of grasping what religion and accounting can teach us, as well as what accounting encompasses, can be found in the undressing of accounting in the light of each religion in turn. The previous chapter undressed each religion, and in the introduction to this book we have already undressed accounting.

V. Joannidès de Lautour, *Accounting, Capitalism and the Revealed Religions*, DOI 10.1007/978-3-319-32333-6_4

This chapter's aim is to re-dress accounting with clothes from the four religions, enabling us to understand what religion can teach us as to the nature of accounting. Through this process, we can understand contemporary accounting issues and debates regardless of current standards or disputes surrounding, for instance, fair value. In other words, the prior study of religious accounting and current investigations of how accounting looks, once dressed up, allows us to see more clearly the whence and whither of major debates surrounding the giving of an account. Under this purview, this chapter shows what can be learnt from each of them separately. Then, a broader discussion of accounting is undertaken, theorising through the joint lessons learnt from the four religions. Lastly, as accounting is understood as a means to accountability, a further discussion on the lessons that can be drawn from religious accountability for business organisations is carried out.

1 Lessons Learnt from the Four Religions

Judaism reveals four issues relevant to contemporary accounting practices. Firstly, the notion of balance between commandments revealed by God through the Tablets and actual conduct stresses double-entry thinking. Everything, every item, every activity, every amount of money has a counterpart, nothing existing per se. This leads to the second issue regarding evaluation models. It is obvious that faithfulness and divine commandments cannot be known, measured or valued (Derrida 1994). Evaluation models prove accordingly to be vain and operate at best as theologies or sets of quasi-religious beliefs (Kamuf 2007). Therefore, and consistent with rabbinic literature, only the believer can faithfully identify what the Lord expects from him or her; no intermediary is legitimate to articulate any doctrine of God's will. Thirdly, as individual accounts are not subjected to any human control, God exerts His will on Judgement Day. Subsequent to the examination of the two books, the Lord either rewards the righteous or punishes the wicked. Faithfulness can be found in the fairness of accounts and in the balance of commandments ordered by the Lord and those actually honoured. God's omniscience precludes any cheating. Accordingly, books of accounts appear as a driver of personal life (Schechter 1895). Correlatively, through reconciliation of mankind with divinity, these autobiographic accounts serve as drivers for the morals of people knowing that they will stand trial before God.

Like Judaism, Roman Catholicism reveals the notion of biographic accounts based on balanced double-entry records. Listing sins and confessing them to the priest acting as a surrogate for the Lord were means of providing the clergy with fair accounts. As in Judaism, giving an account contributes to constructing the moral person, while publicity in sacrament accounting reveals a practicality with regard to rewards or retributions on earth. If sacraments are missing, other Catholics can know it and blame the guilty person, which should lead to self-control through subjugation to the rule (Hoskin and Macve 1986; Quattrone 2004). Roman Catholicism reveals the earliest international reporting standards set, enforced and practiced: all congregations worldwide have kept the same records for centuries.

The two books recorded by Muslims reveal the duality of morals: in this life as well as in the next life. When directed at Allah, the *Account of Life* reflects how one's faithful conduct served and honoured Him. On the other hand, the *Account of Transactions* reveals how the individual conducts him or herself vis-à-vis Creation. Whereas in Judaism the former book is kept by the believer, in Islam accounts are recorded by two angels. But, as in Judaism, the believer stands trial before Allah on the Day of Accounts. On that day, consistency of conduct with the orders revealed by the Lord to the faithful believer is appraised. Accordingly, rewards or punishments are not appraised by anyone, but Allah Himself. Contrary to Roman Catholicism, no intermediaries interfere in the construction of the account. The *Account of Transactions* reveals the realm of accounts: giving a fair representation of conduct to external parties. Accordingly, Islam emphasises two major issues in double-entry bookkeeping. Firstly, everything has a counterpart, which the accountant must identify. It is on this sole basis that balances or imbalances can be stressed, rewarded or punished. Correlatively, the second issue is that a counterpart is contingent upon the context in which it is found. This prevents any claim for objective or true value. It stems from this that fair value is what really counts for the accountant. Perhaps, it is the reason why Allah audits these accounts, thus ensuring that values have the appropriate counterpart. It is also probably the reason why Islamic theologies do not seem to impose a priori counterparts or values.

Protestantism reveals the contents of contemporary debates apropos accounting objectivity/subjectivity and the role of criticism. Manifestly, Protestantism resists the logic of Roman Catholicism and returns to the Jewish roots of Christianity (Wax 1960). Hence, Protestantism, by questioning God's hand in clergy evaluation models, reveals the aporetic nature of the Lord and value (Derrida 1992, 1994). Whereas the Catholic clergy claimed a revealed universal truth given through the Magisterium, Protestantism calls for subjective and contingent truths upheld by active Bible reading and prayer. Applied to accounting, these issues reveal the impossibility of objective and true measurements and evaluation models, which does not disqualify bookkeeping. Rather, this should stress the assumptions made by accountants, criticism being a positive quality for the accounting profession (Bourguignon and Chiapello 2005).

While accounting thinking in Judaism remains metaphoric, Islam suggests the most advanced metaphor closest to contemporary accounting. Thereby, records are systematically verified by external actors commissioned by the Higher-Principal, that is: two angels appointed by God. This concurs with Napier's (2009) as well as Haniffa and Habudaib's (2010) view that Islamic accounting has been abundantly disseminated in the Muslim world for centuries through textbooks and doctrines regarding bookkeeping. Roman Catholicism remains in between, more formal than Judaism and less oriented towards direct accountability to God than Islam. In these three religions we can see similarities in a double-entry mode of thinking aimed at unifying God and mankind. Accordingly, accounting technologies are driven by a metaphorical representation of a double-entry mode of thinking aimed at unifying our dual world. How this is achieved and why approaches differ can be understood through differentiated approaches to salvation and definitions of God's gifts and expected returns.

All this shows that within the four religions studied a form of accounting exists, which differs from one belief system to another. It stems from this that a religion's conception of a journey to somewhere is the basis of accounting systems. The generally accepted contents of accounts thus differ accordingly to reflect the emotions mobilised in the pursuit of this

	Biographic accounts	Facet of accounting	Temporality
Islam	Good and bad actions are recorded. Beneficiaries therefrom or casualties are accounted for as counterparts	Joint audit (two angels) Two books of accounts reconciled AGM-like on the Day of Accounts	Unto death (Day of Accounts)
Judaism	Performed and neglected duties are recorded in distinct two books. Both must coincide on the Judgement Day.	Account of day-to-day management Self-evaluation of personal dashboard contents	Unto death (Judgement Day)
Protestantism	God's blessings and thankfulness	Contingent management accounting Impossible intermediary between the believer and the Higher-Principal	After the second birth
Roman Catholicism	Souls and sins Souls and sacraments	Mechanism of standard-setting GAAPs Accounting for intangibles	Unto death (perpetual rent for the Church)

Fig. 4.1 The different facets of accounting through the four religions

ultimate goal. As the contents are different, their meaning to the faithful person is peculiar to his or her religion. Judaism and Islam emphasise that accounting for how duties ordered by the Lord are performed influence believers' day-to-day conduct, while in Roman Catholicism the institutionalisation of sacramental accounting serves to control ones' conduct. All told, the four religions highlight four different facets of accounting, as per the below table (Fig. 4.1):

It stems from these differentiated approaches to Salvation and paths to God that differentiated rules and routines surround accounts of everyday life. In Roman Catholicism and Islam, books are kept by external bodies. In the former case, the clergy does account for and control everyday conduct, while in the latter, two angels keep records of activities as suggested by God. The Lord ultimately verifies them on the Day of Accounts. In Judaism, the believer records his or her own account in a direct relationship to the Lord. However, on Judgment Day God audits records of life to appraise that they are balanced, thus imposing a format on the believer's accounts. This reveals that rules and routines are contingent upon and construing of the goal pursued and the journey thither. Yet, rules and routines in the keeping of accounts always imply reconciliation, verification and certification, be it in Judaism, Roman Catholicism or Islam. In the latter case, the methods and evaluation models employed seem to be contingent upon what God orders to His flocks.

2 Implications for Contemporary Accounting

The four cases demonstrate the construction of a logical whole and the capability of naming its features objectifying the world's two parts. In so doing, accounting, though very loose or informal (metaphoric in the case studies), starts being systematic, at least for the accountable self who interiorises its dimensions. It is only when the language and logic of accounting and reporting are appropriated that rules can be enforced to move on to the fair representation of one's conduct and achievements for the sake of one's stakeholders.

2.1 World Dualism as Accounting's Grounds

What is central to the four religions and, consequently, crucial to accounting, is how world dualism is solved through accounting in different contexts and why solutions may differ from one setting to another. Within the four religions studied, a form of accounting exists which differs from one belief system to another. It transpires from the three religions that the book itself is not understood in a uniform way: God is jealous in Judaism, punishes Original Sin in Roman Catholicism and is a synonym of justice in Islam. This means that reality is contingent upon subjective representation of the meaning attached to it. That is, ways of pleasing God and salvation differ accordingly: a jealous, repenting or just God does not save believers in the same way.

Concurring with the idea of the world's dualism, we can see the reach of God and mankind for contemporary accounting. Traditionally, as with Roman Catholicism, the business world has been seen as divided into funders and managers. Their relationship has been said to be resting upon information asymmetry. This has given rise to agency theory as well as annual reports, interim reports and the need for auditing records as a way of reconciling these two parties (Power 2003, 2009). As there is no standard for the content and shape of annual reports there is still room for making them operate as metaphors with icons, heroes, facts and stories readers can retain (Davison 2004, 2010, 2011; Quattrone 2004). The entire story of actions undertaken—mergers and acquisitions or new markets gained—provides organisational discourses with some coherence and consistency. These enable us to grasp the bigger picture of the path taken (McKernan and Kosmala 2004). A form of objectification commences when, falling into the public domain, these accounts can be appropriated by anyone. The crossing of people's subjectivities reifies and makes records as well as stories the truth for everyone. Funders and managers can then be reconciled through the representation of organisational deeds and achievements in financial terms, following either rules or accepted principles that make the whole intelligible (McKernan 2007; McKernan and Kosmala 2007).

Over time, world dualism has been considered more complex, dividing economic and non-economic items (Bebbington and Gray 2001; Gray 1992, 2002, 2006, 2010; Gray et al. 1988; Quattrone 2004). At the non-economic end, social and environmental accounts initially formed another dualism. This seems to have been solved through the merging of corporate social responsibility (CSR) disclosures as to give a consistent representation of the organisation's conduct (Cho et al. 2012; Cho and Patten 2013). Such reports make public achievements through photographic representation of orphanages built or evidence of depollution campaigns. Despite endeavours from the GRI or other international bodies at enforcing organisations to adhere to their standards, organisational reporting and disclosure seem to remain dual. Subsequently, there is to date no working representation of communion between economic and non-economic concerns. This teleoaffective structure could be found in current discussions around the making of integrated reporting, reuniting financial and CSR disclosures through a single technology (Frías-Aceituno et al. 2013; García-Sánchez et al. 2013; IIRC 2011; Tregidga et al. 2014).

Irrespective of whether this dualism is resolved or not, the traditional separation of financial accounting (disclosure) from management accounting constitutes another dualism that still exists. As textbooks usually prescribe, disclosure addresses the bottom line's constituencies and is aimed at showing how earnings are formed. Conversely, management accounting accounts for what counts as strategic and can serve for day-to-day management (Parker 2002b). Seemingly, as with integrated reporting, financial and management accounting has not yet been unified, although the XML-XBRL project is pursuing this teleoaffective structure. To date there do not appear to be any clear routines or rules that enable us to solve this dualism. Hence, the journey is unfathomable until rules so arise as to enable representation through fully integrated data (Alles and Debreceny 2012; Dunne et al. 2013; Liu et al. 2014; O'Riain et al. 2012).

2.2 Religious Accounting's Influence on Business Accountability

In today's private companies, it is generally accepted that an account is given to those who entrust their monies to an organisation. Although this latter is often presented as a principal, we prefer relating it to the term 'Higher-Principal' (Laughlin 1996). This label is less suggestive of any systematic temptations to cheat the principal on the grounds of information asymmetry. The Higher-Principal presides over the traditional principal and has the potential to investigate the truth and so interrogate the agent in order to get the amount of information he or she deems satisfactory. While the notion of principal places the account demander in a position of weakness vis-à-vis the agent, that of Higher-Principal positions him or her in a situation of exerting the power of demanding information and sanctioning the agent if not fulfilled (Joannidès 2012; Laughlin 1996).

In a private, listed company, it is commonly agreed in the literature that the principal, or the Higher-Principal, is the collection of stockholders and that their expectations are to be fulfilled. Yet, the notion of stockholders and their expectations may vary. For instance, in family businesses, stockholders, generally company founders, might expect to perpetuate their business and undertake projects aimed at this. In private equity, stockholders are considered investors with a limited time horizon, therefore favouring investments that give returns within their time frame; such investors might ignore long-term productive investments.

This allows us to understand why the contents of accounts and recording procedures differ from one religion to another. The Higher-Principal is not conceived of similarly, so that His requirements cannot be exactly the same. In Judaism, what matters to God is that the believer accounts for the performing of all duties as ordered. Salvation can be gained only through this. In Catholicism, God cannot be known in person, which legitimates the clergy to act as surrogate for Him in determining what He expects through sacrament and sin accounting. Lastly, Islam is constructed of both, so that two angels record how the Sharia's five pillars are honoured. In private companies, differentiated understandings of the agency relationship between managers and stockholders can lead to differentiated forms and contents for accounts. Some only disclose annual reports whilst others also disclose CSR reports. Some disclose interim figures whilst others do not.

3 Lessons for Contemporary Accountability

3.1 Accounting's Raison d'Être Revisited

Research into linkages between accounting and religion reveals the impossibility of applying any traditional theoretical frameworks borrowed from neoclassical microeconomics. First of all, as showed in the four religions, there is no principal–agent relationship as generally observed in functional organisations. If such were the case, God would be the principal and the believer the agent. This would contradict a major religious assumption that God is omniscient.

Rather, God operates as an omniscient Higher-Principal that cannot be cheated. In return, the believer blindly entrusts his or her life to God without knowing in advance what the Lord is doing with it.

Albeit, it is never admitted that a believer would try to control God. Such a thing is practically impossible and theologically a contradiction of God's nature. Moreover, the notion of God has different understandings in each religion. In Judaism, God verifies the accounts on Judgement Day. In Roman Catholicism priests account for them and audit until the believer passes on. In Islam, God accounts and audits the work done by angels. The notion of God itself is a social construct, as practicing the relationship to the Lord has been resting on subjective representations of attached meanings.

Different understandings of stockholders in today's private companies might lead to multiple relationships between managers and fund providers. Accordingly, agency relationships should be viewed as a social construct just like God's identity. Relevant to contemporary accounting research is that accounting serves to reconcile God and mankind as well as managers and stockholders.

Whilst such approaches tend to assume that management's role consists of diminishing conflicts of interest and information asymmetry that employee situations could create, the four religions highlight the need for theories of management legitimacy. In the context of religion, a minister is supposedly coaching his or her flocks, knowing that these have an individual and direct relationship with the Higher-Principal. Hence, those faith managers supposedly render an account of their capabilities to their flocks. Whilst business managers are chosen by the board of directors acting as deputy Higher-Principals, ministers are to be admitted as such by their people. Hence, it does seem that religion and accounting are open for borrowings from alternative frameworks, such as Sen's capability approach.

At this stage, and regardless of the literature addressing linkages between accounting and religion, it appears that accounting comprises an infinite set of technologies aimed at discharging accountability to a Higher-Principal. The four religions elicit the idea of accountability operating as a moralising practice. As God already knows, the believer is to be honed to him or herself by producing a righteous version of him or herself. This can be easily translated to business organisations where accounting serves accountability, both resting upon a form of trust and confidence as well some ethics and morals (Bridgman 2010; Dukerich et al. 2000; Gambling 1977; Gibson 2000; Guidi et al. 2008; Humber 2002; Knights and Vurdubakis 1993; Natoli 2008; Nyberg 2008; Shaw 2003). Therefore, it is now crucial to understand the lessons contemporary business accountability can learn from this.

3.2 Contemporary Accountability as Fidelity to the Event

In order to effectively learn from religious accountability, it is crucial to understand the mechanisms at play in the relationship of demanding and giving accounts, be this in any of the four religions or in a business organisation (Joannidès and McKernan 2014). This common mechanism can be conceived as 'fidelity to the event' (Badiou 2001, 2003, 2007).

According to Badiou, accountability practices are the offspring of an event that changed the face of the world and altered its functioning.

> The event is attached, in its very definition, to the point in which the historicity of the situation is concentrated. Every event has a site which can be singularized in the historical situation [...] It is not because the site exists in the situation that there is an event. But, *for* there to be an event, there must be the local determination of a site (Badiou 2007, pp. 178–179).

Altering the world order of functioning in the future, the event must be locatable in space and time and its actors must be identifiable. An event is generally past (Jesus' death and resurrection) but can be a future promise (the return of the Messiah in Judaism). It just cannot be synonym of present time, precisely because we cannot know whether it is the event in that case, namely because we cannot yet name it. As a result, in his lectures and public appearances, Badiou often warns that global warming is not an event and thus cannot be the basis for an ethics of the environment. In order for such an accountability to be possible, a traceable and identifiable event must be found.

Central to Badiou's philosophy are the ideas that accountability lies in fidelity to the event admitted as true and that truth is not an outcome but a procedure of its dissemination as such. The event is meant to be first individually encountered and accepted as a truth before being shared with others. When shared with others, this witness is harbingered by an apostle (Badiou 2003, p. 45). Jesus Christ's overall message was appropriated by Saint Paul, who had never seen him but had a direct revelation of this truth from God (see Acts). Before him, all other apostles partook in the placement-into-circulation of Jesus' death and resurrection.

Fidelity to the event therefore 'is the work of a militant' and definitely has a political dimension (Badiou 2007, p. 329). The best-known militant thus far has been Saint Paul, the only apostle who never met Jesus. Saint Paul indeed shows us that commitment to the truth event (Jesus' resurrection leading to a new world) cannot be based on proof of any form: 'Christ is precisely incalculable' (Badiou 2003, p. 50).

Grounded in witnessing to an individual encounter (Badiou 2003, p. 66, p. 103), the causative event must have the potential to be reiterated (Badiou 2009, p. 10). As with Paul's conversion to Jesus' new church (Badiou 2003, pp. 17–18), the Christian has a new birth through faith, which iterates Jesus' resurrection (Badiou 2003, p. 45, p. 60). Likewise, the Muslim can iterate the second birth of the Prophet with his or her conversion to Islam and recurrent witnessing thither. This said,

> faith cannot be confused with mere private conviction [...] The reality of faith is an effective declaration, which, with the word "resurrection", utters that life and death are not ineluctably distributed as they are in the "old man" (Badiou 2003, p. 88).

This means the event is perpetuated through the action of witnessing to it before the rest of the world at all times, because 'without fidelity, that declaration is useless' (Badiou 2003, p. 91).

Therefore, the apostle or the militant 'must be accountable only for what others see and hear, which is to say, his declaration' (Badiou 2003, p. 51). In other words, accountability appears as the twofold fidelity to the event. The militant is accountable to those who made the event happen (to Jesus and later on Saint Paul) by steadily reminding of event contemporaneity and pertinence.

Firstly, as they are harbingers of the event, fidelity commits the militant to ensuring its perpetuation (and reiteration) in its aftermath. This must be showed in their daily conduct whereby, confronted with dilemmas, they are expected to ponder what Jesus (Mohammed, Ali or Abraham) would have done in a similar situation and to behave accordingly themselves. If nobody speaks for the event, it will fade as though it had never happened, the world continuing to evolve on its own. This point is backed-up with the argument that Jesus Christ's resurrection would have been ignored if no Christians had spoken for it (Badiou 2007, p. 26). And this, continues Badiou, denies the event its miraculous and overhuman nature. Badiou (2007) calls this a paradox but seems to relate it to an aporetic accountability of the apostle before the event.

Secondly, the apostle is also accountable to the audience they are addressing. He or she is expected to share this unutterable utterance and the depth of event implications with others who have not as yet been exposed to it. Therefore, as with Jesus and then Paul, they must deploy a sort of 'narrative accountability' (Ricœur 1955, 1991). Here, telling the ineffable is the utmost difficulty confronting them. Rather than just telling of the event, later apostles are to conduct a life faithful to the truth event and speaking for it, being fair heirs of those who made the event happen in the past and organised its aftermath. In other words, as with the dissemination of the truth, apostolic accountability lies in witnessing to the event and its changing of our lives since it happened. Failing to behave in accordance with what I think the actor in the event would have done in a similar situation denies it its ethical significance. If nobody eventually abides by the event and makes it part of their day-to-day life, this event is not worthy of any consideration.

3.3 Fidelity to the Event in Business Organisations

Rather than making very general and generic claims apropos business accountability, this section shows three situations derived from the observation of accounting and religion where accountability appears as fidelity to the event: fair trade, the World Wide Web and innovation.

Such is the case of fair trade as a new way of promoting good in the business environment (Moore 2004; Nicholls 2010; Reed 2009).

Nowadays, fair trade constantly convokes Max Havelaar, the hero of Multatuli's 1860 novel written in reaction to Dutch government policy in the Java colony. Havelaar fought the government, who were promoting the growing of rare and expensive produce, such as sugar or cocoa, rather than rich and well-feeding grains, such as rice or sunflowers (Multatuli 1860). The event is Havelaar's uprising, which transgresses the economic order of the time. Multatuli was his first apostle and militant as evidenced in the novel he wrote, as a sort of gospel. Havelaar has since been resurrected in Mexico in 1980, witnessed to and perpetuated through the creation and diffusion of the well-known eponym fair trade label (Audebrand and Pauchant 2009). Fair trade promoters and actors nowadays constantly ponder what Havelaar would have done in a similar situation as theirs and are expected to behave accordingly, whilst the what is doing this good is commonly accepted within that community. Hence, fair trade can apply universally and unambiguously within that community.

A similar phenomenon can apply to the World Wide Web where ethical concerns relate to finding a balance between the free open source model, privacy and intellectual property (Al-Rafee and Cronan 2006; Bakker (de) and Hellsten 2013; Block 2004; Brenkert 2009; Charters 2002; Choi and Berger 2009; Clark and Roberts 2010; Cohen-Almagor 2012; DeLorme et al. 2001; Freestone and Mitchell 2004; Goode and Cruise 2006; Grabner-Kräuter 2009; Gupta et al. 2004; Hamilton et al. 2009; Le Menestrel et al. 2002; Loughran 2005; Maury and Kleiner 2002; Miller and Wekcert 2000; Pagallo and Durante 2009; Palmer 2005; Weijters et al. 2013; Xiaohe 2006; Yang et al. 2009). It is well-accepted within the IT community that the World Wide Web owes its development and reach to Linus Torvalds' subversion of the established order (Raymond 1999). The event can be located in 1985 when the first open source version of the Linux kernel was released. Whilst software development thus far had been proprietary and secret, Torvalds made his own operating system public and open. His subversion allowed for the sharing of data using the Internet. According to Raymond (1999), the world community of hackers and programmers has witnessed to Torvalds' views, by diffusing the open source (GNU) model and making software accessible to the public. More recently, some other major players have claimed Torvalds' legacy, transgressing in their time the established order and causing a revolution on the Internet. Some of them are Larry Page at Google (Jarvis 2011; Vise 2008), Jeff Bezos at Amazon (Stone 2014) or Mark Zuckerberg with Facebook (Kirkpatrick 2011). So far did these new business heroes transgress the established order one day, that Android is a portable version of Linux designed for mobile devices. As of today, discussions around privacy on the Internet, ownership of personal data or copyright raise major ethical dilemmas. According to Badiou's philosophy, an ethics of the Internet should lead anyone involved to ponder what Torvalds would have done in response to these problems and remain committed to doing the good he has always done to the IT community.

Beyond just the IT community, a similar ethical pattern can be identified in the field of innovation with Steve Jobs' legacy (Blumenthal 2012; Dormehl 2013; Watson 2014). In the 1980s, Jobs wanted to challenge the established order. In the first place, he wanted to make computers the available for everyone and not just professionals or hackers. This implied he needed to programme a user-friendly operating system and associated software. At a second stage, he transgressed the seriousness of computers with fancy designs, commencing with the eMac and eBook. At the same time, he decided to challenge the established order relating to music and portable devices by creating the first format for dematerialised pieces (mp3). The iPhone came as a transgression of the order where mobile devices had a keyboard and served just to give and receive calls, which was followed by the iPad challenging the order of laptops. As Jobs' biographers unanimously highlight, Apple's founder has been and still is very influential over innovation in numerous companies outwith IT. He is considered a revolutionary whose apostles are in the first place Apple's fans but also other CEOs impressed by his success and who take inspiration from him. That is, a new philosophy of innovation was created: more than the mere technical aspects of a product, what seems to count is user-friendliness associated with design and regular upgrades and updates. Hence, nowadays, an ethics of innovation in whatever company could consist in pondering what Jobs would have done in a similar situation.

Conclusion

Today's main accounting and accountability debates are inherited from the book's four religions. Each monotheism emphasises a different facet of accounting and accountability. Notwithstanding differences, they have all sought to develop double-entry bookkeeping as a moralising practice ultimately aimed at discharging accountability to a Higher-Principal. In today's business organisations, accountability cannot be reduced to the mere giving of a financial account. In its moralising dimension, contemporary accountability operates as answering the question of how the organisation's militant would have reacted in a similar situation and how we could ensure fidelity to this. That is, with God and their prophets, the book's four religions show a meta-path to requiring accountability. This necessitates the identifying of the Higher-Principal, and his or her expectations as well as how he or she would have behaved if confronted with the same concerns as us. This means there is no one way to discharge accountability but as many as there are organisations and Higher-Principals. Thence, reporting standards, especially if reaching internationally, will necessarily prove to be problematic here or there.

Bibliography

Alles, M., & Debreceny, R. (2012). The evolution and future of XBRL research. *International Journal of Accounting Information Systems, 13*(2), 83–90.

Al-Rafee, S., & Cronan, T. (2006). Digital piracy: Factors that influence attitude toward behavior. *Journal of Business Ethics, 63*(3), 237–259.

Audebrand, L. K., & Pauchant, T. C. (2009). Can the fair trade movement enrich traditional business ethics? An historical study of its founders in Mexico. *Journal of Business Ethics, 87*, 343–353.

Badiou, A. (2001). *Ethics: An essay on the understanding of evil*. London: Verso.

Badiou, A. (2003). *Saint Paul: The foundation of universalism*. Stanford, CA: Stanford University Press.

Badiou, A. (2007). *Being and event*. London: Continuum International Publishing.

Badiou, A. (2009). *The logics of worlds: being and event II*. London: Continuum.

de Bakker, F. G. A., & Hellsten, L. (2013). Capturing online presence: Hyperlinks and sematic networks in activitst group websites on corporate social responsibility. *Journal of Business Ethics, 118*, 807–823.
Bebbington, J., & Gray, R. (2001). An Account of Sustainability: Failure, Success and a Reconceptualization. *Critical Perspectives on Accounting, 12*(5), 557–588.
Block, W. (2004). The "digital divide" is not a problem in need of rectifying. *Journal of Business Ethics, 53*, 393–406.
Blumenthal, K. (2012). *Steve Jobs—The man who thought differently*. London: Bloomsbury Publishing.
Bourguignon, A., & Chiapello, E. (2005). The role of criticism in the dynamics of performance evaluation systems. *Critical Perspectives on Accounting, 16*(6), 665–700.
Brenkert, G. (2009). Google, human rights, and moral compromise. *Journal of Business Ethics, 85*(4), 453–478.
Bridgman, T. (2010). Beyond the manager's moral dilemma: Rethinking the 'ideal-type' business ethics case. *Journal of Business Ethics, 94*(2), 311–322.
Charters, D. (2002). Electronic monitoring and privacy issues in business-marketing: The ethics of the doubleclick experience. *Journal of Business Ethics, 35*, 243–254.
Cho, C. H., Guidry, R. P., Hageman, A. M., & Patten, D. M. (2012). Do actions speak louder than words? An empirical investigation of corporate environmental reputation. *Accounting, Organizations and Society, 37*(1), 14–25.
Cho, C. H., & Patten, D. M. (2013). Green accounting: Reflections from a CSR and environmental disclosure perspective. *Critical Perspectives on Accounting, 24*(6), 443–447.
Choi, C., & Berger, R. (2009). Ethics of global internet, community and fame addiction. *Journal of Business Ethics, 85*(2), 193–200.
Clark, L., & Roberts, S. J. (2010). Employers' use of social networking sites a socially irresponsible practice. *Journal of Business Ethics, 95*, 507–525.
Cohen-Almagor, R. (2012). Freedom of expression, internet responsibility, and business ethics: The Yahoo! saga and its implications. *Journal of Business Ethics, 106*(3), 353–365.
Davison, J. (2004). Sacred vestiges in financial reporting: Mythical readings guided by Mircea Eliade. *Accounting, Auditing & Accountability Journal, 17*(3), 476–497.
Davison, J. (2010). [In]visible [in]tangibles: Visual portraits of the business Élite. *Accounting, Organizations and Society, 35*(2), 165–183.

Davison, J. (2011). Barthesian perspectives on accounting communication and visual images of professional accountancy. *Accounting, Auditing & Accountability Journal, 24*(2), 250–283.

DeLorme, D. E., Zinkman, G. M., & French, W. (2001). Ethics and the internet: Issues associated with qualitative research. *Journal of Business Ethics, 33*, 271–286.

Derrida, J. (1992). Post-scriptum: Aporias, ways and voices. In H. Coward & T. Foshay (Eds.), *Derrida and negative theology* (pp. 283–323). New York: State University of New York Press.

Derrida, J. (1994). *Specters of Marx: The state of the debt, the work of mourning, and The New International.* New York: Routledge.

Dormehl, L. (2013). *The Apple revolution: Steve Jobs, the counterculture and how the crazy ones took over the world.* London: Virgin Books.

Dukerich, J. M., Waller, M. J., George, E., & Huber, G. P. (2000). Moral intensity and managerial problem solving. *Journal of Business Ethics, 24*, 29–38.

Dunne, T., Helliar, C., Lymer, A., & Mousa, R. (2013). Stakeholder engagement in internet financial reporting: The diffusion of XBRL in the UK. *The British Accounting Review, 45*(3), 167–182.

Freestone, O., & Mitchell, V. W. (2004). Generation Y attitudes towards e-ethics and internet-related misbehaviours. *Journal of Business Ethics, 54*, 121–128.

Frías-Aceituno, J. V., Rodríguez-Ariza, L., & García-Sánchez, I. M. (2013). Is integrated reporting determined by a country's legal system? An exploratory study. *Journal of Cleaner Production, 44*(0), 45–55.

Gambling, T. (1977). Magic, accounting and morale. *Accounting Organizations and Society, 2*(2), 141–151.

García-Sánchez, I.-M., Rodríguez-Ariza, L., & Frías-Aceituno, J.-V. (2013). The cultural system and integrated reporting. *International Business Review, 22*(5), 828–838.

Gibson, K. (2000). The moral basis of stakeholder theory. *Journal of Business Ethics, 26*, 245–257.

Goode, S., & Cruise, S. (2006). What motivates software crackers? *Journal of Business Ethics, 65*(2), 173–201.

Grabner-Kräuter, S. (2009). Web 2.0 social networks: The role of trust. *Journal of Business Ethics, 90*(4), 505–522.

Gray, R. (1992). Accounting and environmentalism: An exploration of the challenge of gently accounting for accountability, transparency and sustainability. *Accounting, Organizations and Society, 17*(5), 399–425.

Gray, R. (2002). The social accounting project and Accounting Organizations and Society Privileging engagement, imaginings, new accountings and pragmatism over critique? *Accounting, Organizations and Society, 27*(7), 687–708.

Gray, R. (2006). Social, environmental and sustainability reporting and organisational value creation?: Whose value? Whose creation? *Accounting, Auditing & Accountability Journal, 19*(6), 793–819.

Gray, R. (2010). Is accounting for sustainability actually accounting for sustainability...and how would we know? An exploration of narratives of organisations and the planet. *Accounting, Organizations and Society, 35*(1), 47–62.

Gray, R., Owen, D., & Maunders, K. (1988). Corporate Social Reporting: Emerging Trends in Accountability and the Social Contract. *Accounting, Auditing & Accountability Journal, 1*(1), 6–20.

Guidi, M. G. D., Hillier, J., & Tarbert, H. (2008). Maximizing the firm's value to society through ethical business decisions: Incorporating 'moral debt' claims. *Critical Perspectives on Accounting, 19*(5), 603–619.

Gupta, P. B., Gould, S. J., & Pola, B. (2004). To priate or not to pirate: A omparative study of the ethical versus other influences on the consumer's software acquisition-mode decision. *Journal of Business Ethics, 55*, 255–274.

Hamilton, J. B., Knouse, S. B., & Hill, V. (2009). Google in China: A manager-friendly heuristic model for resolving cross-cultural ethical conflicts. *Journal of Business Ethics, 86*, 143–157.

Haniffa, R., & Hudaib, M. (2007). Locating audit expectations gap within a cultural context: The case of Saudi Arabia. *Journal of International Accounting, Auditing and Taxation, 16*(2), 179–206.

Hoskin, K. W., & Macve, R. H. (1986). Accounting and the examination: A genealogy of disciplinary power. *Accounting Organizations and Society, 11*(2), 105–136.

Humber, J. (2002). Beyond stockholders and stakeholders: A plea for corporate moral autonomy. *Journal of Business Ethics, 36*, 207–221.

IIRC. (2011). Towards integrated reporting. Communicating value in the 21st century. Discussion paper, available at http://www.theiirc.org/theintegrated-reporting-discussion-paper/ accessed 10 August 2012.

Jarvis, J. (2011). *What would Google do?* London: Harper.

Joannidès, V. (2012). Accounterability and the problematics of accountability. *Critical Perspectives on Accounting, 23*(3), 244–257.

Joannidès, V., & McKernan, J. (2014). Ethics: From negative regulations to fidelity to the event. In P. O'Sullivan (Ed.), *From hubris to disgrace: The philosophy, politics and economics of finance in the 21st century*. London: Routledge.

Kamuf, P. (2007). Accounterability. *Textual Practice, 21*(2), 251–266.

Kirkpatrick, D. (2011). *The Facebook effect: The real inside story of Mark Zuckerberg and the world's fastest growing company*. London: Virgin Books.
Knights, D., & Vurdubakis, T. (1993). Calculations of risk: Towards an understanding of insurance as a moral and political technology. *Accounting Organizations and Society, 18*(7–8), 729–764.
Laughlin, R. (1996). Principals and higher-principals: Accounting for accountability in the caring professions. In R. Munro & J. Mouritsen (Eds.), *Accountability: Power, ethos and the technologies of managing* (pp. 225–244). London: International Thomson Business Press.
Le Menestrel, M., Hunter, M., & de Bettignies, H.-C. (2002). Internet e-ethics in confrontation with an activists' agenda: Yahoo! on trial. *Journal of Business Ethics, 39*, 135–144.
Liu, C., Wang, T., & Yao, L. J. (2014). XBRL's impact on analyst forecast behavior: An empirical study. *Journal of Accounting and Public Policy, 33*(1), 69–82.
Loughran, T. (2005). NASD rule 2110 and the VA Linux IPO. *Journal of Business Ethics, 62*, 141–146.
Maury, M. D., & Kleiner, D. S. (2002). E-commerce, ethical commerce? *Journal of Business Ethics, 36*, 21–31.
McKernan, J. F. (2007). Objectivity in accounting. *Accounting, Organizations and Society, 32*(1–2), 155–180.
McKernan, J. F., & Kosmala, K. (2004). Accounting, love and justice. *Accounting, Auditing & Accountability Journal, 17*(3), 327–360.
McKernan, J. F., & Kosmala, K. (2007). Doing the truth: religion deconstruction justice, and accounting. *Accounting, Auditing & Accountability Journal, 20*(5), 729–764.
Miller, S., & Wekcert, J. (2000). Privacy the workplace and the internet. *Journal of Business Ethics, 28*, 255–265.
Moore, G. (2004). The fair trade movement: Parameters, issues, and future research. *Journal of Business Ethics, 53*, 73–86.
Multatuli, R. P. (1860). *Max Havelaar: Or the coffee auctions of a Dutch trading company*. London: Pinguin.
Napier, C. (2009). Defining Islamic accounting: current issues, past root. *Accounting History, 14*(1/2), 121–144.
Natoli, G. (2008). Augustinian moral consciousness and the businessman. *Journal of Business Ethics, 78*(1–2), 97–107.
Nicholls, A. (2010). Fair trade: Towards an economics of virtue. *Journal of Business Ethics, 92*, 241–255.
Nyberg, D. (2008). The morality of everyday activities: Not the right, but the good thing to do. *Journal of Business Ethics, 81*(3), 587–598.

O'Riain, S., Curry, E., & Harth, A. (2012). XBRL and open data for global financial ecosystems: A linked data approach. *International Journal of Accounting Information Systems, 13*(2), 141–162.

Pagallo, U., & Durante, M. (2009). Three roads to P2P systems and their impact on business practices and ethics. *Journal of Business Ethics, 90*, 551–564.

Palmer, D. E. (2005). Pop-ups cookies, and spam: Toward a deeper analysis of the ethical significance of internet marketing practices. *Journal of Business Ethics, 58*, 271–280.

Parker, L. D. (2002b). Twentieth-century textbook budgetary discourse: formalisation, normalization and rebuttal in an Anglo-Saxon environment. *European Accounting Review, 11*(2), 291–313.

Power, M. (2003). Auditing and the production of legitimacy. *Accounting, Organizations & Society, 28*(3), 379–394.

Power, M. (2009). The risk management of nothing. *Accounting, Organizations and Society, 34*(6,7), 849–855.

Quattrone, P. (2004). Accounting for god: Accounting and accountability practices in the society of Jesus (Italy, XVI-XVII centuries). *Accounting Organizations and Society, 29*(7), 647–683.

Quattrone, P. (2009). Books to be practiced: Memory, the power of the visual, and the success of accounting. *Accounting, Organizations & Society, 34*(1), 85–118.

Raymond, E. S. (1999). *The cathedral and the bazaar—Musings on Linux and open cource by an accidental revolutionary*. Sebastopol, CA: O'Reilly.

Reed, D. (2009). What do corporations have to do with fair trade? Positive and normative analysis from a value chain perspective. *Journal of Business Ethics, 86*, 3–26.

Ricœur, P. (1955). *Histoire et vérité*. Paris: Seuil.

Ricœur, P. (1991). *Du texte à l'action*. Paris: Seuil.

Schechter, S. (1895). Some aspects of rabbinic theology: The "law". *The Jewish Quarterly Review, 8*(1), 1–16.

Shaw, T. R. (2003). The moral intensity of privacy: An empirical study of webmasters' attitudes. *Journal of Business Ethics, 46*, 301–318.

Stevens, D. E., & Thevaranjan, A. (2010). A moral solution to the moral hazard problem. *Accounting, Organizations and Society, 35*(1), 125–139.

Stone, B. (2014). *The everything store: Jeff Bezos and the age of Amazon*. London: Corgi.

Tregidga, H., Milne, M. et Kearins, K. (2014). (Re)presenting 'sustainable organizations'. *Accounting, Organizations and Society 39*(6), 477–494.

Vise, D. A. (2008). *The Google story*. New York: Pan.

Watson, G. (2014). *Steve Jobs—The inspirational life story of Steve Jobs, the fruit company that changed our world*. London: Amazon Media EU.

Wax, M. (1960). Ancient Judaism and the Protestant ethic. *The American Journal of Sociology, 65*(5), 449–455.

Weijters, B., Goedertier, F., & Verstrecken, S. (2013). Online music consumption in today's technological context: Putting the influence of ethics in perspective. *Journal of Business Ethics, 124*(4), 537–550.

Xiaohe, L. (2006). On P2P file-sharing: A major problem—A Chinese perspective. *Journal of Business Ethics, 63*(1), 63–73.

Yang, D., Sonmez, M., Bosworth, D., & Fryxell, G. (2009). Gobal software piracy: Searching for further explanations. *Journal of Business Ethics, 87*, 269–283.

5

A Review of the Literature

As the previous three chapters drew on the lessons the history of capitalism, accounting and religion can teach to contemporary accounting, this chapter reviews the existing literature on the subject. Whilst literature reviews tend to be descriptive and give a snapshot of knowledge on a subject, this chapter sets out to provide the reader with a clear overview of how debates have evolved and knowledge has been advanced. Pursuant of this objective, it first highlights what is known and what needs knowing. It then shows how scholars' religious affiliation influences the way they conduct research on accounting and religion.

This chapter reviews the literature on accounting and religion. In this respect, it follows two major pieces useful to the scholar interested in studying the area (Cordery 2015; Joannidès and Berland 2013). Those merit of those two papers lies in the fact that they are more than mere literature reviews. They also highlight the currents of knowledge debates as well as the behind the scenes academic relationships between authors, hence revealing how publications on accounting and religion were decided upon and prepared. This chapter takes inspiration from those two papers and provides the reader with a twofold review of the literature. Firstly, consistent with Cordery (2015) and Joannidès and Berland (2013), it looks at the state of knowledge and academic interests as well as the evolution of discussions over time. Hence, the reader can discern the types of research questions that are of interest now and those that

V. Joannidès de Lautour, *Accounting, Capitalism and the Revealed Religions*, DOI 10.1007/978-3-319-32333-6_5

are outdated. Secondly, given the peculiarity of a research topic dealing with religion, this chapter also shows how researchers' personal views of religion can impact on their research projects on accounting and religion. For this, some insights from researchers' personal lives and journeys are used but identities are not revealed (as not all authors gave permission to do so). In a nutshell, whether they are an insider or an outsider tends to be central to an author's approach to the topic.

1 The Evolution of Knowledge and Debates

This section borrows from two literature review papers published in *Accounting, Auditing & Accountability Journal* (*AAAJ*) (Joannidès and Berland 2013) and *Accounting History* (Cordery 2015) and sets out to highlight how knowledge and debates relating to accounting and religion have evolved since the publication of Laughlin's (1988) seminal paper on the subject.

1.1 Religion as the Social Context in which Accounting Can Operate

In 1988, Richard Laughlin published one of the very first papers studying accounting in the social context of the Church of England (Laughlin 1988), stressing a triple problem. Firstly, academe's understanding of the interplay between the social and technical aspects of accounting systems appears to be insufficient. Secondly, accounting research needs to be emancipated from Watts and Zimmerman's (1986) Positive Accounting Theory,[1] which requires more interdisciplinary, non-economics-based qualitative research. Thirdly, accounting research in the 1980s was colonised by neoclassical economics and needed plural viewpoints and

[1] Positive Accounting Theory states that accounting research must explain and predict accounting practices.

alternative approaches to problems. Laughlin's (1988) paper was coincidental with an accounting history paper showing how the Shakers have promoted accounting and accountability to be self-sustaining (Faircloth 1988). Although neither of the two papers refers to the other as a first in the accounting literature, both rest upon archival methods intended to show that accounting is not neutral or universal but embedded both within history and a social context.

Both Laughlin and Faircloth expressed the need for research taking into consideration the social context in which accounting operates, suggesting recourse to frameworks borrowed from the social sciences, namely the elementary forms of religious life (Durkheim 1898) and the sacred and the profane (Eliade 1959), authors whose authority in sociology has long been proved, particularly through numerous controversies. Consistent with this call for more social and religious accounting research, Laughlin further developed his point in a paper proposing a model of financial accountability for the Church of England and published in *Financial Accountability and Management* (Laughlin 1990). These three exploratory studies marked the commencement of interest in accounting and religion, by setting empirical bases for such further research.

Whilst Faircloth's (1988) paper has had little posterity, Laughlin's (1988) has been the most influential over accounting research. In 1993, Peter Booth published in *AAAJ* a paper derived from his PhD dissertation in which he sought to evaluate 'the contributions of the extant accounting literature on churches to our understanding of accounting as a situated practice, and to sketch some of the possible parameters of a framework for a research programme to build on the strengths and redress the weaknesses of this literature' (Booth 1993, p. 38). He expressed his willingness to extend what he thought Laughlin had conceptualised as the sacred–secular divide. With help from Laughlin (who examined his dissertation) Booth was obviously interested in behavioural and social aspects of accounting.

> I decided that I wanted to study different ways in which accounting was used and how different approaches to rationality might interact with this [...] My interest here was to give some context structure to my looser ideas

> on modes of rationality. I probably did develop more explicitly the sacred–secular divide phrasing in my thesis as it provided a convenient, if a bit over contrived, means to do this, so off I went.

With help from Laughlin, who later became his examiner, Booth found himself engaged with the idea of an expressive case, in other words a case that would highlight the limits of rational economic approaches. He expressed the need to identify the structural properties of these linkages. Four features of the relationship between accounting and religion emerged: religious belief, organisational members, occupational groups and financial resource pressure (Booth 1993, p. 60). To give these categories a structural dimension, Booth needed to find a meta-label: the sacred–secular divide. He acknowledges:

> My inclination is that the sacred–secular divide phrasing came from Richard [Laughlin], even if I was the first to use it explicitly. It wasn't explicit in his writing, but it probably arose from our discussions about my thesis analysis and how to use ideas from his thesis and papers on the sacred and the profane.

Since Booth's (1993) paper, the sacred–secular divide has continued to be evoked and ascribed to Laughlin (1988), certainly because he remains the founding father of this research community. Laughlin has become so central to the community that every publication on the subject eventually positions itself vis-à-vis this dichotomy (McPhail et al. 2005). Yet, as Laughlin confesses:

> I was concerned then and remain concerned about his structural and static interpretation of what was never meant to be as such. I expressed this concern in my comments on the thesis.

After Booth's (1993) paper, it took almost ten years until accounting and religion attracted new academic interest. Intermittently, economics or finance journals published papers trying to draw on a theology of economic or financial practices (Iannaccone 1995; Oslington 1999). But none of those explicitly referred to Laughlin's (1988, 1990), Faircloth's (1988) or Booth's (1993) papers and concepts.

1.2 Accounting and Religion Extended to Accounting in Nonprofits

Accounting and religion as a research topic gained new academic interest in 2000 when Booth's former supervisor (Lee Parker)[2] and another colleague (Lightbody 2000, 2003) began considering that accounting in churches should not be reduced to linkages between accounting and religion. For them, so doing would systematically lead to positioning accounting and religion vis-à-vis the sacred–secular divide. Therefore, their concern was rather to understand the broader community to which church organisations belong: nonprofits, which had 'been accorded relatively little attention in the accounting and management research literatures' (Parker 2001, p. 321). More specifically, studying planning and control in a religious organisation could contribute to knowledge on management accounting in nonprofits. This refocused research discussions around the dynamics between mission and accounting (Parker 2001, 2002) and the behaviour of financial managers in a nonprofit organisation (incidentally a church setting) in their dual capacity as guardians of organisational resources and mission advocates (Lightbody 2000, 2003). Both Parker and Lightbody studied the case of the Uniting Church in Australia, relevant to accounting in the wider area of nonprofits (Parker 2001, p. 322).

As academic interest had shifted towards an underexplored area, that is accounting in nonprofits, Lightbody (2000, 2003) and Parker (2001, 2002) undertook to inform their studies with grounded theory so as to avoid 'any prior commitment to specific "a priori" hypotheses or pre-existing theories in relation to questions posed of interviewees, other data collection or coding for concept identification' (Parker 2001, p. 324). Both revealed that the sacred–secular divide was not the most suitable approach to the understanding of linkages between accounting and religion. To Parker (2002), most appropriate is a mélange of community culture, resources pressure, consultative bureaucracy and

[2] Lee Parker was Peter Booth's supervisor at the initial stage of his PhD when they were at Griffith University, Queensland, Australia. Then, Parker moved to South Australia and Booth, who stayed at Griffith, was supervised by Craig Littler.

compliance-oriented accounting information. In such a situation, tensions can arise amongst people claiming authority over organisational resources (Parker 2001, p. 323).

For her part, Margaret Lightbody disagreed with Booth's contention that there might be systematic and systemic conflicts of rationality between accounting and religion. Her two papers (Lightbody 2000, 2003) were aimed at showing the fact that guardians of the resources and mission advocates are often the same people, subject to the same rationality, resulting in no systematic tension. She confirms that if there are any tensions, these can be ascribed to misunderstandings surrounding the intertwining and overlapping of these two modes of rationality. Conflicts between accounting and the mission can arise in any kind of organisation where mission and money are balanced (Parker 2002, pp. 72–73).

In parallel with Lightbody and in a different state, Helen Irvine completed her PhD in 1999. One of her examiners was Peter Booth, who eventually influenced her work informed with neo-institutional sociology. Phrased differently from Lightbody's work, Irvine endeavoured to generalise her study as far as possible. She therefore studied 'how accounting can be accomplished in an organisation with a strong spiritual agenda' (Irvine 2002, pp. 36–37). That is, her interest was in how mission and money can be balanced in a religious congregation (Irvine 2005). Combining the concepts discovered by Booth in 1993 with neo-institutional sociology, she considered that, 'if the prevalence of religion and, by extension, the significance of religious organizations, is accepted, then the way accounting is treated in these organizations ought also to reveal, at a profound level, something of the inherent nature of accounting' (Irvine 2005, p. 212).

The academic interest had therefore been redefined so as to make accounting in a church setting appealing to a broader audience, extending its boundaries beyond those only interested in nonprofits. For Irvine, the sacred–secular divide is not the essence of accounting in church settings. She explains this through the fact that the studied denomination's religious belief system accounting is accommodated quite well (Irvine 2005, p. 233). These conclusions concur with those drawn by Lightbody at a similar time and with regard to a different denomination. Whilst Parker and Lightbody studied the Uniting Church in Australia, Irvine focused on the Salvation Army. At this stage, the sacred–secular divide is softly challenged.

1.3 Towards Theological Perspectives on Accounting

Since Lightbody's (2003) and Irvine's (2002) publications on accounting in a church setting, the subject has attracted an increasing academic interest, with authors mainly expressing two concerns. Firstly, new scholars were seduced by the study of accounting and religion as interesting per se. Secondly, researchers were studying accounting and religion in the view of illuminating accounting with fresher or *expressive* insights (Berry 2005).

Parker explains that he observed this in 2002 when his second paper was published in *Management Accounting Research*. He had already considered publishing an *Accounting, Auditing & Accountability Journal* special issue on accounting and religion. For this purpose, guest editors, acknowledged experts in the subject, were contacted. Ken McPhail, who had a special interest in accounting and religion asked his former PhD supervisor, Rob Gray, who was also an *AAAJ* associate editor, to help him prepare such a special issue. McPhail admits that for his very first editorial experience he was happy to have some support from an experienced scholar. The project was well received by Parker, yet McPhail considered that having a theologian on board for this editorial project would enhance the credibility of papers dealing with accounting and religion. Interesting Gorringe, a theologian specialising in theology and economics, was not easy. This latter manifested some reservations regarding the pertinence of studying religion from an accounting viewpoint, as if there were a sort of sacred–secular divide between the two realms. Notwithstanding such reservations, Gorringe eventually joined as a guest editor.

Altogether McPhail, Gorringe and Gray decided that research into accounting and religion should take a decisive turn by addressing theological issues rather than accounting in church organisations. This resulted in a selection of papers dealing with various denominational contexts and theologies. That special issue of *AAAJ* published papers seeking to 'initiate a dialogue between immediacy and eternity' (McPhail et al. 2004,

p. 320), offering theological perspectives supposed to enhance our understanding of accounting in general.

As a result, in studies of accounting, accountability and control in various settings, the authors interested in theological insights into accounting relied on these denominations' very theologies as contextual frameworks. Thence, theological minutes issued by the Anglican Council were the basis for Kreander et al.'s (2004) study of investment practices in the Church of England as well as Berry's (2005) scrutiny of accountability and control in that same church. In other denominations, the writings of the founders enabled understanding of accounting as applied to faith, for example Wesley's theology in the UK Methodist Church (Cordery 2006; Kreander et al. 2004) as well as Ferguson's rule in the Iona Community (Jacobs and Walker 2004), but also William Booth's writings in a study of the Salvation Army (Howson 2005). These theological insights were also expected to enable the theorising of 'how accounting is perceived and [if] it is possible that accounting can be perceived as something sacred' (Jacobs and Walker 2004, p. 362). Studying accounting in a religious context was explicitly directed at finding the position on these ideas in the broader accounting community and in society at large (Jacobs and Walker 2004, pp. 362–363).

In parallel, other authors undertook to use alternative theologies to revisit the conceptual roots of linkages between accounting and religion. In passing, they also refuted the existence of any sacred–secular divide, stressing 'a danger that the model [the sacred–secular divide], which has proved insightful in opening up new perspectives on accounting, might become overly restrictive if its categories are employed in a stringent binary fashion' (McPhail et al. 2005, p. 187). References to the same theologians as in the above selection, such as Wesley (Cordery 2006; Jacobs 2005) or Niebuhr's internal and external history and taxonomy of the relationship between church and society (Hardy and Ballis 2005) were aimed at showing that Booth (1993) referred to the work of Durkheim and Eliade in a way that oversimplified the realm of the sacred and the secular. A former PhD student of Richard Laughlin, Jacobs (2005, p. 190) considered that 'central to a lot of the thinking and research in the area of accounting in religious organisations is the work of Laughlin (1988, 1990) and his distinction between sacred and the secular in the context of the Church of England'. In informal talks, Kerry Jacobs says he rejected a structural approach to accounting and religion, which saw religion as inherently sacred and accounting as inherently secular. The Jacobs and Walker (2004) critique was focused on this structuralist interpretation of the work of Laughlin (who was one of Jacobs' PhD supervisors). However, while Laughlin (1988, 1990) used the term 'sacred and profane' it is Booth (1993) who actually used the terms 'sacred–secular'. Jacobs (2005, p. 193) further extended the critique of a structuralist understanding of secular accounting and sacred religious institutions in a study of the Church of Scotland, where he argued that 'the central issue is how accounting is perceived and understood'. This critique was informed by the earlier work with and ongoing support from Walker, particularly in terms of the historical aspects. This critique of the sacred–secular divide was picked up and incorporated into the ongoing work of Hardy on the Seventh Day Adventist Church (Hardy and Ballis 2005, 2013). Parker, qua his PhD supervisor, has stated in informal talks at Auckland University of Technology and via telephone that he was informed of the direction of the dissertation's engagement. This is confirmed by Irvine and Walker (Hardy's examiners) who were impressed by the quality and timeliness of the developing argument. Apparently such support from more experienced actors in this network enabled Hardy to reframe the knowledge debate through his sharp critique of the divide.

Cordery states that her paper (Cordery 2006) sought to reinforce Jacobs' (2005) critique by showing that Wesleyan theology had historically always accommodated accounting as a device for faithful conduct. It is in this mindset that she supervised Francesca Lim's PhD dissertation (Lim 2013), in which Bonhoeffer's theology informed the notion of accounting for labour. While doing her PhD, she received help from Vassili Joannidès de Lautour who then was chosen to be her external examiner. That is, her work was encouraged to engage in a critique of the sacred–secular divide and in a thorough theological discussion of accounting for labour.

Yet as Walker and Jacobs have said in informal discussions, another major opponent of the sacred–secular divide is Ezzamel, although his works do not explicitly refer to it until 2009:

> These suggestions are in sharp contrast to much of the extant literature on accounting in religious institutions, where the focus is upon functional, housekeeping and monitoring issues with accounting viewed as a profane activity (Ezzamel 2009).

Such reference is made explicit, as though Ezzamel's opposition to the sacred–secular divide was not obvious to all actors in this network. Arguing on the structural properties characterising linkages between accounting and religion, these critics (Ezzamel, Jacobs, Hardy and Ballis, and Cordery) attempted to move the debate on and implicitly suggested that the foundations of today's accounting knowledge are unreliable and call for clarification and correction.

McKernan notes that these critiques on the sacred–secular divide were very promising insofar as they had the potential to instil religion into accounting. Yet McKernan and Kosmala (2007, p. 731) stress a new problem in the evolution of the network and knowledge: theological and sociological approaches had overly focused on accounting in a religious context, neglecting the essence of both accounting on one hand and religion on the other. This point is confirmed by Cordery (2015) who remarks that accounting history research dealing with religion tends to merely describe practices in a certain congregation or denomination with no other contribution to knowledge and little theorising. Therefore, establishing parallels between accounting and religion through Ricœur's hermeneutics (McKernan and Kosmala 2004) or Derrida's deconstruction (McKernan and Kosmala 2007) would highlight commonality in both. Ultimately, if religion is proved to influence accounting, questioning what is their common essence will enhance our understanding of both (McKernan and Kosmala 2004, p. 329, 2007, p. 730).

This led a senior researcher (McKernan 2012) and an emerging scholar (Joannidès 2012) to borrow from Derrida's aporia of responsibility to reveal intrinsic unresolved contradictions of accountability. McKernan (2012) did so through the story of Abraham's responsibility before God. From a similar critical stance, Berry (2005) tried to build on the essence of accountability and control through an expressive case, that is a case revealing features of account-giving not visible in functional settings. Thence, studying the Church of England enabled him to see accountability as a bundle of (religious) covenant, and (legal) constitution and contract. Building on Berry's (2005) work (Berry was his external PhD examiner), Joannidès de Lautour discussed how accountability practices in the Salvation Army have been grounded in an accounting spirituality fostered by the denomination's theology (Joannidès 2009).

These critical approaches reframed and endeavoured to conceptualise the prior critiques on the sacred–secular divide. These publications' aim was to understand how the very essence of accounting on one hand and religion on the other can be so mutually supportive as to make a theory of their intertwining emerge by itself. It is about how they manage to reveal quasi sacred concepts in time and space, considering first, pervasive temporal structures and ritual in corporate financial reporting, and second, the use of icons, particularly visual images which perhaps recall the symbolism of ascension (Davison 2004).

1.4 Back to Accounting History

As demonstrated by Cordery's (2015) literature review paper, research into accounting and religion took a new turn in 2006, since which time more and more scholars have addressed accounting history matters. Yet these papers have not kept the promise to produce major new knowledge. All this started with a paper on non-financial accounting and accountability in the Society of Jesus, at the time of Reformation (Quattrone 2004). In this paper, Quattrone (2004) shows how Reformation fostered new theological developments and a mode of accounting for sins, indulgences and sacraments (Aho 2005). This paper gave birth to another paper showing how the Jesuits influenced the development of accounting's visual forms (Quattrone 2009). Quattrone's papers were motivated by the fact that prior research on accounting and religion

> reinforced the taken-for-granted economic nature of accounting practices [so] little is known about the ways in which research on religious entities may shed new light on the nature of accounting and accountability. Even less is known about the ways in which these organisations can contribute to an understanding of the relations between the emergence of these

> practices and the development of certain organisational forms such as hierarchies, which have proliferated in modern times (Quattrone 2004, p. 648).

In between emergence of those two papers, Carnegie expressed the need for historical perspectives on linkages between accounting and religion that had arisen. This led him, as editor of *Accounting History*, to invite Salvador Carmona as a member of the journal's editorial board to be guest editor of a special issue on accounting and religion. Carmona suggested that Mahmoud Ezzamel should join, which Carnegie accepted. Ezzamel, who had already worked in accounting in the religious context of Ancient Egypt (Ezzamel 1994, 1997, 2005), rejecting the notion of a sacred–secular divide, was naturally sympathetic to the idea. The special issue was to be published in 2006, so the call for papers was published in the *AAAJ* 2004 special issue on accounting and theology. Carnegie indicated that having Parker as PhD supervisor facilitated connections between *AAAJ* and *Accounting History*. Following the talks in Darwin and in a further email, he explains 'the special issue was motivated by a desire to develop an understanding of accounting's past in social organisations, including religious institutions', this being consistent with the interdisciplinary project.

In the 2006 special issue of *Accounting History*, this concern was further emphasised by Carmona and Ezzamel (2006, pp. 117–118) in their editorial. The guest editors stressed a new problem: prior works treated religious institutions as a branch of nonprofits whose sole focus was on Christian churches. The possibilities offered by religion to understand accounting more broadly had apparently been underestimated. This led them to publish papers producing a genealogy of discourses on wealth and the need for accounts in the Bible (Baker 2006) or showing how accountability was conceived by Moses at the time of the Exodus from Egypt (Barlev 2006). They also mobilised papers which showed the functional use of accounting in the Monastery of Silos in Spain (Prieto et al. 2006), as well as in Spanish brotherhoods (Álverez-Dardet Espejo et al. 2006).

Notwithstanding Carmona and Ezzamel's (2006) expressed satisfaction vis-à-vis this special issue of *Accounting History*, Cordery (2015) considers that merely empirical knowledge has been produced in those publications and thereafter, without significantly enhancing our understanding of either accounting or religion. Between 2006 and 2013, as accounting and religion attracted increasing academic attention, contributions to knowledge were following the law of diminishing returns. Therefore, alternative approaches have emerged in reaction to the limits of contemporary research's contributions to knowledge.

1.5 Alternative Theologies as Critical Perspectives on Accounting

A formally critical stance apropos accounting and religion has emerged since the publication of two papers informed by alternative theologies in the *AAAJ* 2004 special issue (Gallhofer and Haslam 2004; Tinker 2004). Tinker, who was already known as a major proponent of Labour Process Theory and Marxist approaches, highlights a new problem:

> More than ever before, religion and Marxism need to suspend their mutual suspicion and join in a careful, interrogation of capitalism. If there is an "idealism" in Marxism, it is something shared by some Christians and Muslims—the ennoblement of Man-on-Earth (Tinker 2004, p. 464).

Thereby, Tinker contributes to the discussion on the linkages between accounting and religion from a historical viewpoint. He finds commonalities between the Marxist, Christian and Islamic critiques of capitalism and subsequent accounts. In personal correspondence, he explains:

> This paper [*the AAAJ* 2004 paper] *is* one of a long series of papers arguing in keeping with Marx's critique of Hegel (Hegel asserted that that God Created Man). Marx famously said that he found Hegel standing on his head and turned him the right way up (Man Created God).

The need for alternative approaches is revealed by Gallhofer and Haslam (2004) who notice that relationships between accounting and religion have been conveyed through mainstream accounting theories and theologies. Therefore, they give voice to subalterns through liberation theology in Latin America. This enables them to confirm that the sacred–secular divide is by no means reserved to the core of accounting and religion but that it also pertains to mainstream research. As critical management scholars, they clearly call for further research embracing alternative views and approaches, highlighting more systematically how theology influences day-to-day accounting practices.

> As liberation theology emphasises different texts to those given more weight by the theological mainstream, so can emancipatory accounting. It can lay stress on some texts more than they have been emphasised to date. A counter-hegemonic reading of mainstream accounting will necessarily also draw attention to its limitations in terms of facilitating emancipatory struggle (Gallhofer and Haslam 2004, p. 395).

Liberation theology is presented as a theology giving hope to and supporting the emancipation of oppressed people. Moerman (2006) finds herself responding to this appeal critically and endeavours to discuss linkages between emancipatory accounting and liberation theory. Thereby, she seeks to further conceptualise Gallhofer and Haslam's (2004) conclusions on liberation theology, deeming the microeconomic ideology underlying accounting inappropriate, as liberation theology does not reveal an ontological opposition to accounting. This point is reinforced by a later study on the biblical jubilee as a theological critique addressed to institutions basing accounting and accountability on economics (Moerman 2008). As showed by Cordery (2015), having papers published both in *AAAJ* and *Accounting History*, Moerman tried to contribute to this dual debate: on the lessons we can learn from the past and on critical insights into accounting and religion.

By transforming Gallhofer and Haslam's (2004) trial study, Moerman (2006, 2008) made Pala Molisa want to further develop and conceptualise accounting's emancipatory project. Building on Gallhofer and Haslam (2004), he sets out to inform emancipatory accounting with an ontology of spirituality rather than a theology or religious doctrine (Molisa 2011). In the same issue of *Critical Perspectives on Accounting* in which Molisa published his paper, Gallhofer and Haslam (2011, p. 506) invite further investigation of these issues:

> Taking seriously spirituality points to a critical theoretical holistic perspective that is enhanced in its richness and concerns: it embraces the inner as well as the external world and it deepens appreciation of emancipation.

What this literature review reveals is the domination of Western theologies and church settings over the field, whilst other contexts have been neglected. Within Christianity, the Church of England and the Uniting Church in Australia have been over-studied until Irvine's (2002) paper on the Salvation Army. Therefore, calls for papers addressing Islamic accounting have been articulated (Napier 2009). Seemingly, this tentative call has received a positive response with the launch of the *Journal of Islamic Accounting and Business Research* in 2010. This new outlet takes for granted that both accounting and Islam are mutually supportive (Hannifa and Hudaib 2010). In parallel with Napier's (2009) tentative definition of Islamic accounting, accounting in Hindu and Buddhist communities was studied (Javayasinghe and Soorbaroyen 2009), the authors underlining that this is the very first study of accounting in a context other than the three monotheisms or Ancient Egypt (e.g. Ezzamel's works).

The evolution and currents of research into linkages between accounting and religion can be understood through authors' personal relationships with the empirical subject matter. In a nutshell, our investigation has revealed that the religious affiliation of researchers has a strong influence on the entire research design.

2 Religious Affiliation's Impact on Accounting Research Projects

Over time, it seems three streams of thought have emerged on accounting and religion. The first one assumes the existence of a sacred–secular divide whilst the second openly and bitterly criticises such a standpoint. Lastly, the third stream presents accounting as a religious practice regardless of discussions about a possible sacred–secular divide. Seemingly, the stream which sees a sacred–secular divide is that of , whilst the one arguing that accounting is a religious practice is that of insiders. At this stage, it may be intuited that such is the case because addressing religious issues is not an incidental choice but can reflect the willingness to witness (Carmona and Ezzamel 2006). We assume here that such interests emerge because scholars have something to say about these issues relating to their own identity. This section shows how the degree of access to or prior knowledge of the field influences how a research project is conceived and constructed. Each of the two streams is presented separately.

2.1 The Sacred–Secular Divide Stream: Outsiders' Insights

Three papers concur about the existence of a sacred–secular divide, all of them written by religious outsiders (Booth 1993; Laughlin 1988, 1990). Another two papers refute the sacred–secular divide but purport to oppose 'storing' and 'shielding' (Lightbody 2000, 2003). While Booth clearly confessed he had no affiliation with his research subject the Church of England, Laughlin apparently did have responsibilities there but then unhappily quit. It does seem that his two papers were written in reaction to his experience. Something similar happened to Lightbody, who had been very active in the Uniting Church in Australia but eventually left after years. Whilst her research project was undertaken when she was still a member, her papers were published after she departed.

The five papers implicitly aim at drawing universal laws with regards to connections between accounting and religion. Endeavouring to arrive at a structuralist theory thereof, those papers view the Church of England as a fixed object seen from outside or above. As objects, these churches are somehow black boxed and regarded in a manner whereby the research can claim to draw universal laws. Different denominations and internal social relations are then approachable by any researcher external to the denomination or congregation.

Questioning the relationships between accounting and the social context of a religious organisation (Laughlin 1988), or the design of accountability in a specific organisation (Laughlin 1990), assumes that a religious setting is specific and does not apply accounting as other organisations do. This is very suggestive of a religious setting being driven by a strong belief system and the honouring of a sacred sanctuary. Similarly, Booth's

(1993) paper sets out to extend Laughlin's conclusions through a conceptual framework explaining the sacred–secular divide. Unsurprisingly, after having defined the notions of guardians and advocates borrowed from Wildavsky, Lightbody (2000, 2003) seeks to examine storing and shielding behaviours of financial managers and subsequent negative reactions from the religious occupational group (p. 158). Common to the five papers is that the question itself tends to assume financial managers are rationality-centric, whereas religious people are driven by non-financial ideologies. Hence, the Uniting Church in Australia is viewed as a black box, in which accounting and religion are intrinsically dichotomised.

The main critics of this stream are Jacobs (2005), Hardy and Ballis (2005) and Cordery (2006), who bitterly denounce the predictability of such research. For those critics, the proponents of the sacred–secular divide implicitly assume that accounting and religion have hermetic typical concerns through the postulate that divinity only lies in the sacred sanctuary whereas accounting is relegated to business-related premises. Thereby, these scholars observed a twofold world ex ante borrowed from Eliade and Durkheim founded upon the following key assumptions. (1) All activities within are necessarily either sacred or secular. (2) Tensions between sacred beliefs and secular activities always occur and cannot be avoided. (3) Sacred beliefs always dominate religious organisations, in particular issues related to money or economic rationality. (4) Operating within society, religious organisations are obliged to embrace its rational and secular practices (Hardy and Ballis 2005, p. 240).

Admittedly, categorisation enabled the treatment of two issues discreetly before combining them. In other words, examining the sacred on the one hand and the secular on the other was necessary to facilitate the understanding of the core question of each, and ultimately the typical question of accounting and religion as new objects of enquiry. In fact, the link between both seems to lie in the divide, which divorces them in lieu of joining them. More specifically, these researchers have emphasised accounting issues while, relatively speaking, leaving religious subjects aside. In other words, they have conducted accounting research in an organisation, which (incidentally?) was a church. Eventually, the concepts used, sacred sanctuary and religious belief system, were defined but treated as fixed objects. With no insights into the specific belief system being brought to the reader, these researchers seem to have behaved as external observers. It is worth recollecting that epistemology research states that observer questions tend to neutralise interactions and objectify an empirical object to arrive at general laws or rules; in other words, such questions reveal realist ontology.

Taking a single-stream reality leads one to consider it as mainstream, characterised by the termination of discussions on its core assumptions and methodologies. Henceforth, conclusions are taken for granted as the expression of external reality, on other words the sacred–secular dichotomy appears as reality to many scholars (McPhail et al. 2004, 2005).

Whatever their label is, the dichotomies stressed between accounting and religion discovered through the systematic a priori construction of categories do not only highlight ontological limitations but also a uniform apprehension of the world. Indeed, scholars who identified a sacred–secular divide implicitly assumed that reality was objectively present in the elementary forms of religious life (Durkheim 1898) or in the segregation of the sacred sanctuary and clergy from the rest of the world (Eliade 1959). This relates to a dichotomy between the sacred and the profane stemming from religious experiences of the individual who enters the sacred sanctuary when he converts to the religious belief system in question. He ascertains that, for the religious person, space is not homogenous; it evidences discontinuities, ruptures: there are parts of space that are qualitatively different from others. On the contrary, for profane experiences, space is homogenous and neutral: no discontinuity qualitatively differentiates its various parts (Eliade 1959, pp. 25–26). Believers conduct themselves as the wardens of the sacred sanctuary, for instance the premises or location in which gods are prayed to and praised. In order to point out the non-homogeneity of space, as experienced by the religious person, one can refer to a banal example: a church building, in a contemporary city. For the believer, that church is part of different space than that of the street where it is located. The gate that opens to the interior conveys a form of continuity but the threshold that separates both spaces (street and church) conveys at the same time the distance between the two modes of being: profane and religious. The threshold is at the same time the boundary that differentiates both worlds, and the paradoxical place where they communicate, where one can move from the profane world to the sacred world (Eliade 1959, p. 28). Henceforth, all their actions in the world belong to the sacred realm, while, on the contrary, the sacred–secular divide was held prior to conversion, conduct therein being profane because it was not directed at the sacred sanctuary.

This led authors to rigidly apply a strong theoretical framework emphasising these divides. Hence, according to Jacobs (2005), the conclusions drawn from these studies arriving at the existence of a sacred-secular divide were expected and made the starting point of these publications. Although Laughlin (1988, 1990) and Booth (1993) found themselves confronted by Jacobs, they never engaged in an academic discussion with him through replies and commentaries. They have eversince let things go. This outsider's viewpoint resulted in the authors working on second-hand empirical material, such as archives or some interviews. As the aim was not necessarily to provide an understanding of the church context itself, this latter was empirically and methodologically black boxed. Dichotomy-based works have recourse to historical (Laughlin 1988; Booth 1993) or verificational (Laughlin 1990; Lightbody 2000, 2003) tools: they observe a sacred–secular divide, because Durkheim (1898) and Eliade (1959) have stated it. If the proponents of this approach do not refer to these authors, they draw on management-centric literature reviews (Booth 1993) wherein prior non-managerial literature is ignored. When they rely on more complex theories, these studies are interview-based and focus on one dimension (conflicts) instead of two (religious accounting and accounting spirituality), capturing people's discourses through tape-recorded interviews structured by the sacred–secular divide (Lightbody 2000, 2003).

Interestingly, in her 2000 publication, Lightbody announces a grounded theory approach as an 'ongoing process of dialogue between the author and the individuals being studied to ensure the resultant understanding did in fact "fit" the phenomenon from which it was derived' (Lightbody 2000, p. 159) crossed with Wildavsky's guardian–advocate model as a meta-theory. We hereby must acknowledge that the consistency of her work with the canons of grounded theory was debated, some arguing that she misunderstood or unduly extrapolated Glaser's and Strauss' ideas (Gurd 2008), others seeing conversely an operationalisation of Strauss' and Corbin's (1994) broad propositions (Joannidès and Berland 2008).

Whoever is right, we must stress the protocols used in the 2000 and 2003 publications: semi-structured interviews, questionnaires and archival work. An outsider's empirical material consists of any type of archives and data giving a glimpse of the general phenomenon addressed and not necessarily its internal construction and interactions. Unlike this stream of thought, the one arguing that accounting is a religious practice rests upon insiders' research questions, empirical material and participative methods.

2.2 The Refutation of the Sacred–Secular Divide: Insiders' Perspectives

This stream of thought comprises of all non-accounting history papers but Cordery's (2006) and Ezzamel's (2009). As Cordery (2015) states, accounting history papers are by definition the work of historians and raise different epistemological questions, which are outwith the scope of this book.

Within this stream of thought, two approaches emerge, both being however manifested in participant questions, in other words questions addressing why and how things are done. Under this purview, the researcher is much inclined to rely on his or her own representation of the field to apprehend interactions.

Those who bitterly critique the sacred–secular divide consider it clear that 'the sacred and the secular are not to be understood as structuralist categories but as individual experiences' (Jacobs 2005, p. 193) and therefore express research questions stressing the analytical framework's inappropriateness. Rather, research questions set out to understand the determinants of planning (Parker 2001) or the means by which planning processes are intertwined with budgetary incrementalism and other controls in a religious organisation (Parker 2002). In these cases, papers read as if the author expected to demonstrate that the relationships between accounting and religion should be explained otherwise than through the sacred–secular divide approach. More explicitly, they question how researchers can apprehend the relationships between accounting and religion without assuming the existence of dichotomies (Hardy and Ballis 2005) or how researchers have created it through performative conclusions (Jacobs 2005). So doing openly challenges dichotomies whose inexistence is, resultantly, assumed.

In all these cases, the religious setting is no longer a black box, but a social body in which people's interactions give evidence of relationships between accounting and religion, which cannot be forecasted. In other words, these publications read like assumptions that a religious setting is created by its members and that understanding its subtleties requires affiliation or at least acquaintance with it. Indeed, in the methodology section of her paper, Irvine (2005, p. 213) declares her membership in the Anglican Church of Australia, while Parker (2001, p. 326) refers to his Christian affiliation apropos understanding the Victorian Synod Church in Australia. Unsurprisingly, Hardy and Ballis have long been affiliated with the Seventh Day Adventist Church. Likewise, Cordery is a member of the New Zealand Methodist Church.

2.3 The Accounting-as-Religious-Practice Stream: Insiders' Insights

Researchers concluding that accounting is a religious practice seem to have considered the congregation studied as a nominal, social ideal construct. Seeking to understand the base of accountability and control in a religious setting (Berry 2005), the biblical foundations of church investments (Kreander et al. 2004) are very suggestive of the church being understood through human interactions, including reflexivity practiced by the researcher. In fact, Berry (2005, p. 256) openly claims that 'he was an actor in the institution [the Church of England] and hence a participant observer', which was expected to provide 'the stimulus for internal and external reflexivity that will be needed to pursue the study' (ibid.). Such reflexivity vis-à-vis the object studied can also be found in intents to understand how religion can influence accounting as fair practice (McKernan and Kosmala 2007), how religious ethics can restore accounting authority over business operations (McKernan and Kosmala 2004) and how accounting can support mission and spirituality in a religious organisation (Howson 2005; Jacobs and Walker 2004). Arguably, such research questions revealed nominalist ontology and were very suggestive of researchers' religious affiliations (McPhail et al. 2005, p. 187).

The discussion of the categories and concepts used by proponents of the sacred–secular divide revealed that 'there is a danger that the model, which has proved insightful in opening up new perspectives on accounting, might become overly restrictive if its categories are employed in a stringent binary fashion' (McPhail et al. 2005, p. 187). Therefore, in doing grounded theory research, Parker (2001, 2002) sought to depart from prior works by adopting a grounded theory approach, which was expected to avoid a priori commitment to hypotheses of theories in relation to questions posed or other data collected. Doing so, he intended to grasp how accounting and planning systems were articulated and implemented in a religious organisation. Consistent with his grounded theory approach, Parker did not rest either upon the sacred–secular divide theory nor its antithesis, but eventually showed its inappropriateness. In other words, Parker established connections between various discourses, archives and practices, showing reality being collectively constructed.

Following Parker, the proponents of accounting as religious practice claim neither external reality nor universal theories but seek to establish interconnections between various perspectives. For them, both accounting and religion are perceived and constructed by the actors themselves and the researcher. As the object includes an infinite number of facets, it requires observation from multiple viewpoints. These can found theoretically in interdisciplinarity and methodologically in crossed methods (McPhail et al. 2004, p. 321). Accordingly, interrelations between the perceptions of accountants, churchgoers, theologians, social scientists, ministers, lay-people and the scholar himself contribute to the construction of the connections between accounting and religion.

Referring to Christian leaders and theologians, such as John Wesley (Jacobs 2005), Richard Niebuhr (Davison 2004; Hardy and Ballis 2005; Jacobs 2005), Dietrich Bonhoeffer (Lim 2013) or William Booth (Howson 2005; Irvine 2002; Joannidès 2012) can lead to believe in greater proximity to object reality because of better knowledge of the religious discipline in question. Such an approach is then accentuated by the participative methods employed to collect and process data. All authors from that stream combined ethnographic and autobiographic accounts and triangulated them with internal documents and some interviews. In fact, the researcher's personal journey was revealed as part of the methods employed. The Australian Anglican Church for eight years (p. 213), where she has been volunteering qua an accountant. Likewise, Berry (2005, p. 256) relies on his membership in the financial board of the Church of England to conduct rich research from a constructionist viewpoint. The others combined and triangulated data collected from their experiences as churchgoers and being financially skilled with internal documentations and interviews (e.g. Parker 2001, p. 321). In a similar vein, Irvine's (2005) paper on the Anglican Church in New South Wales rests upon her husband's ministry therein. But also Joannidès de Lautour (2009, 2012) claims his membership in the Salvation Army to justify the use of ethnographic empirical material and the production of behind the scenes data. Those who do not claim their belonging to the studied organisation combined archival work and interviews (Hardy and Ballis 2005; Jacobs 2005; Jacobs and Walker 2004; Kreander et al. 2004), triangulation between various standpoints and discourses allowing the construction of interactions and interrelations.

Conclusion

Studying accounting and religion is not as peculiar as was in the 1980s. Hence, one cannot claim this is an under-studied topic. Also, this chapter highlights that questioning the existence of a sacred–secular divide between accounting and religion is no longer pertinent today, as a consensus has arisen against this idea. Rather, two types of research are representative for contemporary accounting research discussion: accounting practices in a certain congregation and theological perspectives on accounting. However, thus far, mostly Anglo-Saxon Christian settings have been studied with an emphasis placed on how accounting is practiced within a certain congregation. There is still a need for research bringing newer theological insights into accounting and publications dealing with non-Western contexts.

This chapter also shows how researchers' religious affiliations have a strong impact on how they deal with accounting and religion. Membership in the congregation studied seems to have a significant effect on the articulating of a research question, the adoption and use of a theoretical framework as well as the choice and treatment of empirical material. Although these issues relate to epistemological discussions, this chapter purposefully did not engage in that type of debate, leaving the reader with this responsibility. It does seem that insiders tend to rely on congregations' theology and doctrines to apprehend interactions between churchgoers, ministers and accounting technologies. Contradistinctively, outsiders tend to adopt explanatory theoretical frameworks, archival empirical material and verificational methods. This conclusion is important to scholars interested this topic, because the choice of studying religion is never accidental but tends to reflect willingness to understand, witness to or challenge a certain belief system. Hence, depending on researchers' motivations and personal relation to the field, their project might engage in one or the other direction.

Bibliography

Aho, J. (2005). *Confession and bookkeeping—The religious, moral, and rhetorical roots of modern accounting*. New York: State University of New York Press.

Álvarez-Dardet Espejo, C., López Manjón, J. D., & Sánchez-Matamoros, J. B. (2006). Accounting at the boundaries of the sacred: the regulation of the Spanish brotherhoods in the eighteenth century. *Accounting History, 11*(2), 129–150.

Baker, R. (2006). Towards a genealogy of wealth through an analysis of biblical discourses. *Accounting History, 11*(2), 151–171.

Barlev, B. (2006). A biblical statement of accountability. *Accounting History, 11*(2), 173–197.

Berry, A. (2005). Accountability and control in a cat's cradle. *Accounting Auditing and Accountability Journal, 18*(2), 255–297.

Booth, P. (1993). Accounting in churches: A research framework and agenda. *Accounting Auditing and Accountability Journal, 6*(4), 37–67.

Carmona, S., & Ezzamel, M. (2006). Accounting and religion: A historical perspective. *Accounting History, 11*(2), 117–127.

Cordery, C. (2006). Hallowed treasures: Sacred, secular and the Wesleyan Methodists in New Zealand, 1819-1940. *Accounting History, 11*(2), 199–220.

Cordery, C. (2015). Accounting history and religion: A review of studies and a research agenda. *Accounting History, 20*(4), 430–463.

Davison, J. (2004). Sacred vestiges in financial reporting: Mythical readings guided by Mircea Eliade. *Accounting Auditing and Accountability Journal, 17*(3), 476–497.

Durkheim, E. (1898). *The elementary forms of religious life*. Oxford: Oxford's World's Classics.

Eliade, M. (1959). *The sacred & the profane—The nature of religion—The significance of religious myth, symbolism, ritual within life and culture*. San Diego, CA: Harcourt Brace Jovanovich.

Ezzamel, M. (1994). The emergence of the 'accountant' in the institutions of Ancient Egypt. *Management Accounting Research, 5*(3–4), 221–246.

Ezzamel, M. (1997). Accounting, control and accountability: Preliminary evidence from Ancient Egypt. *Critical Perspectives on Accounting, 8*(6), 563–601.
Ezzamel, M. (2005). Accounting for the activities of funerary temples: The intertwining of the sacred and the profane. *Accounting and Business Research, 35*(1), 29–51.
Ezzamel, M. (2009). Order and accounting as a performative ritual: Evidence from Ancient Egypt. *Accounting Organizations and Society, 34*(3–4), 348–380.
Faircloth, A. W. (1988). The importance of accounting to the Shakers. *Accounting Historians Journal, 15*(2), 99–128.
Gallhofer, S., & Haslam, J. (2004). Accounting and liberation theology: Some insights for the project of emancipatory accounting. *Accounting Auditing and Accountability Journal, 17*(3), 382–407.
Gallhofer, S., & Haslam, J. (2011). Emancipation, the spiritual and accounting. *Critical Perspectives on Accounting, 22*(5), 500–509.
Gurd, B. (2008). Remaining consistent with methods? An analysis of grounded theory research in accounting. *Qualitative Research in Accounting and Management, 5*(2), 122–138.
Hannifa, R., & Hudaib, M. (2010). The two Ws of Islamic accounting research. *Journal of Islamic Accounting and Business Research, 1*(1), 5–9.
Hardy, L., & Ballis, H. (2005). Does one size fit all? The sacred and secular divide revisited with insights from Niebuhr's typology of social action. *Accounting Auditing and Accountability Journal, 18*(2), 238–254.
Hardy, L., & Ballis, H. (2013). Accountability and giving accounts: Informal reporting practices in a religious corporation. *Accounting Auditing and Accountability Journal, 26*(4), 539–566.
Howson, K. (2005). The Salvation Army: Aspects of their financial administration: Success and failure. *Managerial Auditing Journal, 20*(7), 649–662.
Iannaccone, L. R. (1995). Voodoo economics? Reviewing the rational choice approach to religion. *Journal for the Scientific Study of Religion, 34*(1), 76–88.
Irvine, H. (2002). The legitimizing power of financial statements in The Salvation Army in England, 1865–1892. *Accounting Historians Journal, 29*(1), 1–36.
Irvine, H. (2005). Balancing money and mission in a local church budget. *Accounting Auditing and Accountability Journal, 18*(2), 211–237.
Jacobs, K. (2005). The sacred and the secular: Examining the role of accounting in the religious context. *Accounting Auditing and Accountability Journal, 18*(2), 189–210.
Jacobs, K., & Walker, S. P. (2004). Accounting and accountability in the Iona Community. *Accounting Auditing and Accountability Journal, 17*(3), 361–381.

Javayasinghe, K., & Soorbaroyen, T. (2009). Religious 'spirit' and peoples' perceptions in Hindu and Buddhist relgiious organizations. *Accounting Auditing and Accountability Journal, 22*(7), 997–1028.

Joannidès, V. (2009). *Accountability and ethnicity in a religious setting: The Salvation Army in France, Switzerland, the United Kingdom and Sweden.* Unpublished PhD dissertation, Université Paris Dauphine, Paris.

Joannidès, V. (2012). Accounterability and the problematics of accountability. *Critical Perspectives on Accounting, 23*(3), 244–257.

Joannidès, V., & Berland, N. (2008). Reactions to reading 'remaining consistent with methods? An analysis of grounded theory research in accounting'—A comment on Gurd. *Qualitative Research in Accounting and Management, 5*(3), 253–261.

Joannidès, V., & Berland, N. (2013). Constructing a research network—Accounting knowledge in production. *Accounting Auditing and Accountability Journal, 26*(4), 512–538.

Kreander, N., McPhail, K., & Molyneaux, D. (2004). God's fund managers: A critical study of stock market investment practices of the Church of England and UK Methodists. *Accounting Auditing and Accountability Journal, 17*(3), 408–441.

Laughlin, R. (1988). Accounting in its social context: An analysis of the accounting systems of the Church of England. *Accounting Auditing and Accountability Journal, 1*(2), 19–42.

Laughlin, R. (1990). A model of financial accountability and the Church of England. *Financial Accountability and Management, 6*(2), 93–114.

Lightbody, M. (2000). Storing and shielding: Financial management behaviour in a church organization. *Accounting Auditing and Accountability Journal, 13*(2), 156–174.

Lightbody, M. (2003). On being a financial manager in a church organisation: Understanding the experience. *Financial Accountability and Management, 19*(2), 117–138.

Lim, F. (2013). *The economic entity and accounting for labour: Insights from Dietrich Bonhoeffer (1906–1945).* Wellington, New Zealand: Victoria University of Wellington.

McKernan, J. F. (2012). Accountability as aporia, testimony and gift. *Critical Perspectives on Accounting, 23*(3), 258–278.

McKernan, J. F., & Kosmala, K. (2004). Accounting, love and justice. *Accounting Auditing and Accountability Journal, 17*(3), 327–360.

McKernan, J. F., & Kosmala, K. (2007). Doing the truth: Religion—Deconstruction—Justice, and accounting. *Accounting Auditing and Accountability Journal, 20*(5), 729–764.

McPhail, K., Gorringe, T., & Gray, R. (2004). Accounting and theology, an introduction: Initiating a dialogue between immediacy and eternity. *Accounting Auditing and Accountability Journal, 17*(3), 320–326.

McPhail, K., Gorringe, T., & Gray, R. (2005). Crossing the great divide: Critiquing the sacred secular dichotomy in accounting research. *Accounting Auditing and Accountability Journal, 18*(2), 185–188.

Moerman, L. (2006). People as prophets: liberation theology as a radical perspective on accounting. *Accounting, Auditing & Accountability Journal, 19*(2), 169–185.

Moerman, L. (2008). The biblical jubilee: old wineskin for a new wine? *Accounting History, 13*(2), 207–226.

Molisa, P. (2011). A spiritual reflection on emancipation and accounting. *Critical Perspectives on Accounting, 22*(5), 453–484.

Napier, C. (2009). Defining Islamic accounting: Current issues, past root. *Accounting History, 14*(1/2), 121–144.

Oslington, P. (1999). Theological economics. *International Journal of Social Economics, 27*(1), 32–44.

Parker, L. D. (2001). Reactive planning in a Christian bureaucracy. *Management Accounting Research, 12*(3), 321–356.

Parker, L. D. (2002). Budgetary incrementalism in a Christian bureaucracy. *Management Accounting Research, 13*(1), 71–100.

Prieto, B., Maté, L., & Tua, J. (2006). The accounting records of the Monastery of Silos throughout the eighteenth century: The accumulation and management of its patrimony in the light of its accounts books. *Accounting History, 11*(2), 221–256.

Quattrone, P. (2004). Accounting for god: Accounting and accountability practices in the Society of Jesus (Italy, XVI-XVII centuries). *Accounting Organizations and Society, 29*(7), 647–683.

Quattrone, P. (2009). Books to be practiced: Memory, the power of the visual, and the success of accounting. *Accounting Organizations and Society, 34*(1), 85–118.

Strauss, A., & Corbin, J. (1994). *Grounded theory methodology: an overview*. In N. K. Denzin & Y. S. Lincoln (Eds.), *Handbook of Qualitative Research* (pp. 273–285). Thousand Oaks: Sage.

Tinker, A. M. (2004). The enlightenment and its discontents: Antinomies of Christianity, Islam and the calculative sciences. *Accounting Auditing and Accountability Journal, 17*(3), 442–475.

Watts, R.L. & Zimmerman, J.L. (1986). *Positive Accounting Theory*. New York: Prentice Hall Inc.

6

An Example—The Salvation Army

This chapter gives an example of research that has been undertaken on accounting and religion, taking account of the main critiques usually addressed to such research. The construction of an accounting spirituality and the practice of faith-based double-entry bookkeeping is revealed through the case of the Salvation Army. Though Christian, this case does depart from mainstream Western theologies. Moreover, the example developed in here is not that of financial reporting in one more congregation, as already done in previous studies but addresses an accounting spirituality in a different setting. Pursuant to its founder's social project, the Salvation Army theology borrows from liberation theology and takes some of its structure from the Society of Jesus, whilst it claims its grounding in the Old Testament, the Jews' Bible. Two types of account are brought to light: the balancing of Faith and Action on one hand and of Witness and Collection on the other.

Whilst Chaps. 2–5 highlight why research into accounting and religion is important and how it has evolved thus far, this part of the book provides the reader with a working example of how such research can be conducted. Under this purview, it builds on the Salvation Army case divided into three separate sections—each of them addressing a different issue explicated early on. This case study has three merits. Firstly, it rests upon a specific theology. Secondly, this case offers some functional accounting issues but also new accounting matters. Thirdly, it presents

V. Joannidès de Lautour, *Accounting, Capitalism and the Revealed Religions*, DOI 10.1007/978-3-319-32333-6_6

most of the issues addressed in the previous chapters in practice, while otherwise several settings would have been needed to cover its entirety.

The Salvation Army was founded in 1867 in London's poor districts by a Methodist pastor, William Booth. Following his recognition of the fact needy people were perceived as troublemakers, he quit the UK Methodist Church and decided to found a congregation to provide them with 'soup, soap and salvation'. According to Salvationist theology, salvation is offered for free by God to everybody, provided they respond to His calling (Booth 1890). To this end, the Salvation Army furnishes temporary emergency aid (soup) with its 'soldiers' offering food to the poor so that they do not starve and may hear the Gospel (Sandall 1947, 1950, 1955).

Today, this mission has been expanded to provide broader material emergency support, including catering, clothing and temporary accommodation (Winston 2000). As soup meets immediate needs, soap allows social 'outcasts' to recover their dignity and hygiene as human beings, so that nowadays, soap includes all kinds of social work aimed at restoring people's humanity (Brigou 1994). In this dual capacity as a denomination and registered charity, the Salvation Army has historically organised its activities around spiritual coaching and social work such as soup kitchens, social housing support, training and coaching holiday camps (Watson 1964; Wiggins 1960, 1968). According to its founder's theology, churchgoers must be involved in their church's social work either as volunteers or employees (Booth 1890; Joannidès 2012). Social work with no religious foundation would make very little sense to the Salvation Army, as this would not match its identity. In turn, spiritual coaching with no social work would also not be consistent with the Salvation Army's ethos.

To socialise outcasts, the Salvation Army has adopted a military structure based on titles and hierarchy in the belief that strong 'martial' discipline alone can provide people with clear benchmarks for behaviour (Booth 1890). A general elected by commissioners selected from an officer corps (the clergy) has traditionally headed the organisation. He or she appoints territorial commanders to administer territories and commission on his or her behalf officers (majors, captains and lieutenants depending on their duties) to enlist soldiers attending corps (congregations) and working or volunteering in homes managed by the Salvation Army. Nowadays, its martial structure enables it to be responsive and send volunteers wherever any distress is made known (Winston 2000). For instance, the Salvation Army military structure enabled it in 2010 to send 285,000 meals to Haiti within two days, following the earthquake which devastated the island (Salvation-Army 2010). Such a structure has enabled the organisation to accumulate substantial know-how and expertise in the provision of social work, so that numerous governments in the world rely on its ministers, social workers and employees to delineate national social policies.

Since it was first launched in 1865, the Salvation Army has been operating in 117 countries. It currently has five million soldiers with ten million churchgoers congregating in 77,000 congregations worldwide. Consistent with its theology, the Salvation Army is a registered charity in these countries and aids 50 million needy people every year (Salvation-Army 2012). In its role as a major partner of governments, the Salvation Army is financed mostly through public funding, amounting up to 76 % of its resources in countries like France where public money amounts c. 98 million euro for a total of c. 130 million euro (Salvation-Army 2012). As such it is not surprising that accountability for the Salvation Army in France is firstly directed towards the French Government. However the Salvation Army's identity as both a denomination and registered charity raises numerous legal and control issues.

This chapter provides an example of how theology can be translated into accounts of day-to-day conduct. The case developed is that of the Salvation Army's international accountability system and the needs for accounts of oneself.

1 Capitalism and Accounting Spirituality in the Salvation Army

As Berry (2005) notes, the accountability system of a church rests upon numerical figures. These evidence the honouring of the covenant made with God. Given the theological assumption of God's omniscience, these accounting figures merely bring to bear the lenses of the denominational doctrines. The accounting system is contingent upon the very doctrines of the church. The Salvation Army delineates its theology into numerical accounting figures, as a counsellor of the general states:

> The Salvation Army is weberian. Our spirituality is strongly grounded in accounting and in the development of capitalism. Like the Jesuits, we have developed a capitalistic bookkeeping of our theology and of our faith.

Seemingly, his words do combine economic and religious rationality. Moreover, he seems to take both rationalities as equal and connects them to the development of capitalism. To Weber, the development of capitalism has led to seeking for the accumulation of profit. Economically, this has led individuals to calculate any action and decision in terms of costs and benefits. Their rationality would lead them to undertake only what is profitable. On the other hand, religious rationality is connected to the religious beliefs system and to the doctrines of the congregation. Whereas systematic economic rationality can be universally applied, religious rationality can be systematic within one given beliefs system.

The Methodist notion of payback can help understand why the counsellor of the general connects the spirituality of the Salvation Army to the development of capitalism. The historians of the Salvation Army consider that it was born with and has expanded alongside capitalism (Booth 1890; Coutts 1973, 1986; Sandall 1947, 1950, 1955; Wiggins 1960, 1968). In its beginnings, William Booth recruited his sheep among the poor working class in East London. Since then, it has been composed mainly of social outsiders. Nowadays, these are unemployed or homeless people, in other words people who have not been able to benefit from capitalism. Rather, the members of the Salvation Army have traditionally been people who have suffered due to capitalism (Walker 2001). The Salvation Army has therefore existed thanks to capitalism and some of its social outcomes. To some extent, one could consider that they are twin historical movements. Therefore, understanding the relationship between capitalism and accounting rationality can help understand the interplay between capitalistic accounting and the spirituality of the Salvation Army.

The counsellor to the general applies the debit–credit reasoning to the spirituality of the Salvation Army.

> When we count God's blessings one by one, we account for them as for credit. We are indebted for them in the usage that we make thereof. The counterpart of our credit records is our actual conduct. Then, we are supposedly to balance both counterparts in our day-to-day life.

The Salvation Army's essence has been to critique the excesses of capitalism. At the same time as the organisation operates as a fence to various dysfunctions of capitalism, it borrows from it its tools and has adopted many of them. Incorporated in a capitalistic society, the Salvation Army also speaks its language.. Reversely, capitalism has been able to appear as the main support of its critics. The accounting spirituality of the Salvation Army stresses the main strength of capitalism: it integrates and subordinates its critics and dysfunctions (Boltanski and Chiapello 1996). So does accounting. Although it has been a capitalistic control device, it has become part of the denominational spirituality. Accounting thinking has pervaded spiritualties for a long time already.

Quattrone (2009) observes that the balance sheet of a religious order, when directed at God, discloses invisible items, such as divine grace (faith) and souls (people). It is the very issue of the accounting system that it transforms them into numerical figures that become visible and therefore understandable to anyone. Saying this, Quattrone does not differ much from Weber's (1922) notions of religious spirituality. To the latter, the invisible can be regarded as credit, whereas the visible is accounted for as debit. The link between both happens to be the whatever numerical figures employed.

Faith and other gifts from divine grace are recorded as credit. On the other hand, actions and their outcomes are accounted for as debit. Faith is given, whereas actions mirror the usage made thereof. The accounting spirituality suggests that debit and credit records should be balanced. Actions should fairly mirror the faithfulness of the believer; and reciprocally, his faith should lead him to undertake the subsequent actions. Having said that, one could think that the maximisation of the total account would result in maximising the value of God's kingdom. As credit records are either exogenous or hardly measurable, debit records would be expected to be maximised. The maximisation of God's kingdom would consist of accumulating as much as possible in the *action* records. In order to avoid any ambiguities, the territorial commander in France makes the issue explicit. What counts is the maximisation of the credit records, in other words what is originated by God.

Paris: Territorial Headquarters, 15 November 2005, 9:30 a.m.

This morning, the territorial commander, his cabinet and the heads of departments are having an extraordinary meeting on faith and action. Briefly, the territorial commander leads the service. Then, he speaks out:

'By order of the General, I have to freeze any new investment. Not that we have got into financial trouble. We do have money. But our work does not reflect who we are, even though it is a very good job. In fact, I we will maintain our projects in progress. But, we will open no more homes. Even, we will have to sell or to close some of them. Our concern is to balance our action with our faith.'

I can hear some protests in the hall. The secretary for social work seems not to agree on the diagnostic of the commander.

'In fact, we have to focus on our core activities: proximity faith-based social work. Instead of recruiting more and more external people, we will endeavour to involve our soldiers in our diaconal project. Rough social work is not the Salvation Army, be it a very high quality work.'

The incident above evidences that the issue is not the maximisation of actions (that is of God's total balance sheet). Rather, it is the balancing of faith by actions. For that purpose, the general ordered that the territorial commander downsized the Salvation Army. It is likely that the total of actions was due to the fact of unfaithful people, in other words non-soldiers. On balance with this, the faith records would remain unchanged. This would result in an unbalanced 'God' account. The utilisation of faith (actions accounted for as debit) would be higher than faith itself (accounted for as credit). Therefore, downsizing the French affiliate of the Salvation Army would lead to actions mirroring faith's reality. This raises two questions: how to measure faith and how to account for it? This is what the next sections will address (Fig. 6.1).

In the analytic representation of the categories, sub-categories are labelled as follows:

F: faith
E: employment (action device n°1)
V: volunteering (action device n°2)
W1: social work (witness device n°1)
W2: demonstrations before civil society (witness device n°2)

	Debit	Credit
Employment	E	
Volunteering	V	
Faith		F
Faith & Actions		
Social work (employment or volunteering)	W1	
Demonstrations before civil society	W2	
Wearing of the uniform	W3	
Collection of souls		C1
Collection of supports		C2
Witness & Collections		
Faithful conduct	Conduct = sum (E:W3)	
God's kingdom		God = F + C1 + C2
Total	Conduct = God	Conduct = God

Fig. 6.1 Comprehensive God account

W3: wearing of the uniform (witness device n°3)
C1: collection of souls (contribution to God's kingdom n°1)
C2: collection of supports (contribution to God's kingdom n°2)

By order of the general, the international headquarters set the accounting standards that every territory and every parish are to apply. Moreover, on the occasion of periodical audits, they control the regularity of the records in respect to the constitutional norms. The incident below summarises this.

Territorial Headquarters, Stockholm, 13 September 2007, 3:00 p.m.

> Today, I am having a meeting with the chief accountant of the Swedish territory. First, she apologises for not having very much time. Indeed, she is busy because internal auditors of the international headquarters are due to come in two weeks' time.

> 'Every two years, the IHQ sends us internal auditors. They control the regularity of our records. They are not interested in the annual reports that we disclose to governments. In fact, they focus on the respect of the Salvation Army accounting standards, which are specific to us. Parishes report their accounts to the Territorial Headquarters. We consolidate them and then we report them to the International Headquarters. They consolidate them and disclose them in the yearbook. Attention! The yearbook is something other than the annual report. In brief, the yearbook focuses on our three core accounts.'
>
> Her assistant specifies that
>
> 'The IHQ consolidates everything, but our financial accounts. In fact, they are more interested in our actual balancing of the "God" account. Imagine that parishes report their "Faith & Action" account to the Secretary for Social work, their "Witness & Collection" account to the Secretary for Evangelisation and their "Donations" account to the Secretary for finances.'

At first glance, it seems that the accounting norms of the Salvation Army would support the international expansion of the organisation. The territorial headquarters issued international accounting standards and procedures (Howson 2005; Irvine 1999, 2003; Irvine and Gaffikin 2006; Larsson 2002a, b, c). Thereby, the system of demanding and giving of reasons for conduct can be the same in all territories. The issue in the consolidation of the accounts facilitates controls exerted by the international headquarters. The harmonisation of accounting figures highlights any deviation from the norm (Bourguignon and Chiapello 2005). Organisational accounting norms would insist on what really counts. Obviously, the accounting norms of the Salvation Army support a managerial accounting system. Church leaders may make decisions on the basis of what makes sense for the organisation. It is clear that what counts is the delineation of faith in any actions, and the secretary for finances in Switzerland confirms this.

> The International Headquarters consolidates all accounts, but financial. They are not interested in them, insofar as they do not mirror our spirituality in actions.

Management accounting in a church setting is not necessarily cost based. Accounting calculations produce knowledge about faith in practice. That is what supports managerial decision-making in the case of the Salvation

Army. For that purpose, controls are exerted hierarchically. Parishes report their accounts to the departments of the relevant territorial headquarters. The secretary for evangelisation is concerned about calculations on witness and on soul collections. The secretary for social work is concerned about measurements of embodiment in the completion of the organisational social project. The secretary for finances is concerned about the donations of soldiers. As all these issues are intertwined, the division heads working together on the management of the denomination.

The centre (international headquarters) plays a central role in the accounting process. They set the standards and are an accounting regulator, like the general in the Society of Jesus. Parish accountants report their local accounts to the territorial headquarters on a periodic basis. There, all parish accounts are consolidated and then reported to the international headquarters (Howson 2005; Irvine 1999). As decision-making is located at the international headquarters, the territorial headquarters merely collect and gather accounting figures and instructions from the general. Periodically, auditors from the international headquarters control the conformity of records to the standards. Throughout the process, the international headquarters impose their controls. Accounting standards operate as distant controls, inasmuch as they are applied indifferently by all peripheral affiliates (Quattrone and Hopper 2005). Subsequently, the combination of centralisation with distant and imposed controls characterises bureaucratic systems (Uddin and Hopper 2001). In the vertical accounting relationship, information is reported from the parish to the territorial headquarters. Like in the Society of Jesus, the accountability system of the Salvation Army is shaped by a bureaucratic and hierarchic accounting system. This is consistent with its military structure. The general orders; officers manage soldiers who execute. The next three sections detail how these norms are accounted for at the most local level.

2 Balancing Faith and Action

The last three articles of the covenant made with God explicitly draw on the programme of the Salvation Army to ensure His kingdom, that is social work. Given that social work stands in the covenant, it is ranked like any obligation required by God, as part of the religious belief system. This means that upholding the Salvation Army is part of God's kingdom on earth. It is the visible accountability of the church and its members that the project be completed. Therefore, individuals are committed thereto as a finality. By promising to help the needy and the disadvantaged, the Salvationist promises that he will be involved in social work, in other words in the denominational project.

2.1 Evaluating and Recording Faith

Since 2006, the leaders of the Salvation Army have benefited from territorial congresses to recall the action dimension of the covenant. The incident below is an example of this.

Stockholm, Jakobskirkan, youth congress of the Salvation Army, 30 June 2008, 2:00 p.m.

> I am attending the congress of the Salvation Army. We are gathered in the largest room of Jakobskirkan. A plenary session entitled 'Faith and Action' is about to start. Two hundred and fifty teenager Salvationists from all over Sweden surround me. I can hear: 'Faith and Action? What does that mean?'
>
> When the session starts, the minister in charge of social work comes onto the stage and addresses us.
>
> 'William Booth, founder of the Salvation Army, was very much concerned with the social involvement of his soldiers. It is part of our faith and of our duties as Christians that we are involved in the social work of the Salvation Army.'
>
> After that introduction, the minister calls two people onto the stage to testify what 'Faith and Action' means for them.
>
> A female soldier takes the microphone:
>
> 'Halleluiah!'
>
> 'Halleluiah!' the assembly replies.
>
> She speaks then out:
>
> 'I am now a social worker in a home of the Salvation Army. Thanks to God, this has been possible because the Headquarters granted me a scholarship for my education and my training programme. Thanks to their

financial support, I was able to be a full-time student and to get a degree in social work. It is obvious to me that I offer God the skills acquired.'

'Halleluiah!'

Thereupon, the minister calls a male soldier to the microphone:

'I graduated in accounting from a business school. In my curriculum, I had to do a three-months internship. I did it at the accounting division of the Territorial Headquarters. They gave me the opportunity of gaining professional experience. Immediately after his, I could find a position in a company. I am so thankful to God for this first experience that I have been volunteering as the accountant of my parish since then. To me, Faith and Action means offering the Lord my skills on my free time.'

'Amen!'

Apparently, faith precedes actions. Soldiers receive divine grace, then they demonstrate faith and thankfulness to God for that.. Therefore, Weber considers that faith is to be accounted for as credit. It is a liability of the believer: he is indebted to God for it and is expected to employ it accordingly. In fact, as the minister suggests, faith is not to be appraised. A counsellor of the general admits that

> We cannot appraise the faithfulness of our soldiers. At best, we can assume it, insofar as they made a covenant with God on their free will. However, what we can appraise is the consistency of their actions with their faith.

Faith is the self's personal relation to God and is located in the believer's very core of intimacy. Nobody else is able to enter this intimate place. Accordingly, it is impossible to measure someone's faithfulness. In a religious setting, faith is assumed. Measurements can only be attempted through manifestations thereof. At best, one can appraise the manifestations of faith, not faith itself. What can be appraised and measured is how faith is employed. Given the religious belief system and the normative scheme of the Salvation Army, the working unit for faith is the embodiment in social work. Given their assumed faith, soldiers are expected to do social work. Likewise, social work within the Salvation Amy is assumed to evidence faith and ministers are to recall this regularly to soldiers. One day, when I was preparing the parish newsletter, the minister had an argument with a soldier.

> As a soldier of the Salvation Army, you must be involved in our social work. How can you pretend that you are a faithful soldier and that you love your neighbour, if you do not participate in soup distribution? I know that you have plenty of time to devote to set your faith into actions. Go and get registered for the one or the other activity of the week.

Manifestly, the counterpart of faith is a set of actions. To Weber (1922), the respect of the religious law is recorded as for debit. It draws on the issue of the evaluation thereof. Two questions can be posed: 'what actions?' and 'how much?' The answer to the first question lies in the announcements: any of the weekly activities of the Salvation Army, be they collective or individual. The answer to the second question is less obvious. How much involvement is expected from the believer refers to what his faith commands.

The anecdote reported here suggests that the Salvation Army might intervene in the evaluation of faith. Its leaders suggest practicalities and support employment and volunteering. The young lady instances employment as a social worker, whereas the young man exemplifies the offering of one's skills as a volunteer. As she was interested in social work, the Salvation Army paid for her education and training. She then offers them back in the capacity of an employee. On the other hand, the young man was first given the opportunity to offer his accounting skills to his church on the occasion of a training period. He then paid this back by offering his skills to his parish in the form of a volunteer accountant. In one case, the believer offers her skills on a full-time basis and perceives a compensation for that. In the other case, the churchgoer offers his skills gratuitously on a part-time basis. Whatever the practicality of embodiment chosen, the soldier decides beforehand how much time and money he will devote to the completion of the denominational project. The territorial commander in France confirms that the case observed in Sweden is not isolated. Rather, this responds to the current needs of the Salvation Army.

> In Sweden, they are very good at supporting young people in their projects and at gaining fair employees or volunteers. These last few years, the

> Salvation Army in France has endeavoured to do the same. We have been funding degrees for social workers or for home directors. For instance, Alain graduated as a specialised social worker. We have also funded the CAFDES[1] for Pierre [...] In the same vein, we have been offering training periods to some of our soldiers. Erika worked at the communication department for four months before finding a position in a publishing company [...] Of course, by doing this, we expect our soldiers to use the acquired skills within the Salvation Army, whatever they do [...] I think it normal that we support vocations.

Actions are based upon the self-appraisal of the best faithful utilisation of God's gifts. This corresponds to the highest value for assets gained with faith. a soldier is indebted for his basic training and pays it back on his own. He self-prices what he pays to the Salvation Army and self-evaluates both counterparts of his accounts. The degree of involvement in the social programmes of the Salvation Army depends on the self-evaluation of his faith and of what it orders. It is assumed the order is different from zero and that if he is not involved, he cannot be deemed as a faithful person.

By supporting candidates to enter into volunteering or employment, the Salvation Army individualises their accountability. Evidently, they demonstrate that faith can be neither appraised nor controlled. As the very intimacy of the believer, faith is the locus of accountability to oneself par excellence. On the other hand, when supporting manifestations of faith, the leaders of the Salvation Army can know who is particularly faithful. As they know these volunteers and these employees, they can scrutinise their conduct easily. In fact, church leaders can closely control their actions. A second way of suggesting faithful conduct consists of recalling how faith shall be manifested in the Salvation Army. The minister explains that

> It is part of our faith and of our duties as Christians that we are involved in the social work of the Salvation Army.

[1] The CAFDES is a mandatory degree to become the director of a social services home in France.

He speaks of Christian duty in the context of the Salvation Army. He equates being a Christian with being a Salvationist; in fact he recalls that the Salvationist is a Christian who belongs to a specific denomination with a special purpose. It is because the attendee is a Christian that his duty is to be involved in the social work of the congregation. The use of the term 'duty' draws on normative issues in being a Christian/Salvationist.

Saying what God's will is and what is to be done, the ministry for communication and publications speaks out on a practical feature of the religious belief system. In fact, the congress attendees are not able to distinguish between being a Christian and being a Salvationist. God's will leads the church leader to give reasons for doing social work. In fact, by combining God's will and the denominational approximation thereof, the church promotes social work to the religious belief system. As part of the religious belief system, that organisational truth operates as a norm for conduct, something which is not up for discussion. The counterpart of being committed to God is involvement in social work. The covenant establishes a normative gateway between faith and action in everyday life. The duty declaration accentuates the signification of social work. It is the parishioners' accountability to God that they comply with the commandments of the religious belief system.

The faithful embodiment in social work does not differ much from other religious denominations. It is like in the Society of Jesus (Quattrone 2004), the Church of England (Berry 2005; Kreander et al. 2004), the UK Methodist Church (Kreander et al. 2004), the Church of Scotland (Jacobs 2005), the Iona Community (Jacobs and Walker 2004) and the Victorian Synod Church (Parker 2001).

2.2 Employment

The aforementioned anecdote suggests that full-time employment and ministry are the highest value given to faith's commandments. In those cases, faith commands full-time actions within the church. Ministers are everlastingly thankful to God and devote their life to the religious belief system (Berry 2005; Irvine 2005; Jacobs 2005; Kreander et al. 2004;

Laughlin 1988, 1990; Lightbody 2000, 2003; Parker 2001; Raymond 1976; Thompson 1991). Employees price their liability as full-time involvement in actions. When employed by the Salvation Army, soldiers do not have to account for their actions at the parish level. It is rather the territorial headquarters that account for social work. The territorial commander in Switzerland explains that

> When employed by the Salvation Army, our soldiers do render accounts of their actions only to myself. Together, we set their provisional actions. And then we verify what they actually did. Parishes are not involved in that relation.

To some extent, the accountability relation in the case of Salvationist employees is based upon a contract. Hence, it operates like in the Church of England (Berry 2005) where faithful conduct is appraised as the capability of honouring the contract. In that case, it is not the quantitative work that counts as faithful conduct but rather the capability of fulfilling one's duties. Therefore, Since 2002 the Salvation Army has developed quality programmes, as the secretary for social work in Sweden notes.

> There is no doubt that our soldiers are faithful social workers. However, it is crucial that their work is of high quality. Faithfulness consists of being a good professional.[2]

The Salvation Army accounts for employees and for ministers as well as for all other members. The statuses of minister and of employee allow distinguishing various degrees of embodiment in social work. The faithfulness of employees can neither be questioned nor addressed. The accounting system acknowledges them as faithful people and their practical involvement in social work is accounted for in terms of their actual position and duties. Like in the Church of England (Berry 2005), these are formalised in a negotiated labour contract.

---

[2] The present book does not address the quality management issue. Albeit, mentioning it sheds light on the transformation of the covenant into a contract, when soldiers are employees (full-time actions). The model of evaluation is then specific to their status.

2.3 Volunteering

The present section introduces the techniques and procedures employed to account for volunteering. First, the secretary for announcements recalls all actions of the parish. For each of them, Salvationists are expected to have performed. On the other hand, the minister himself recalls the anchorage of those actions in faith but he also suggests that faith commands such actions.

Actions Hope project

> On 7 September 2006, when I open my personal mailbox, I find a post from the territorial headquarters. It is a letter with a form that every Salvationist is called to fill in.
>
> The text of the letter is:
>
> 'Dear Salvationist,
>
> By order of the General, soldiers are called to be involved in the diaconal project of the Salvation Army. For that purpose, we are developing projects based upon the actual skills on which we can count within the Salvation Army. This new approach of our work is called Actions Hope project. Thereby, the programmes of the Salvation Army match more closely what your faith commands.
>
> To facilitate it, please fill in the joint form fairly.
>
> God bless your involvement.
>
> The Territorial Commander.'
>
> On the next page, I find the form. It is composed of four sections.
>
> In the first section, I am to fill in my qualifications and the practical skills that they developed. I may enter four items.
>
> In the second section, I am to specify how I could volunteer on the basis of my skills.
>
> In the third section, I specify the needs I have observed in my borough.
>
> In the fourth section, it is suggested that I estimate what actions I can undertake to respond to these needs and how much time I should give.
>
> I filled in the form and returned it instantly.

The Actions Hope project evidences that the Salvation Army encourages skill-based social programmes. In this project, Salvationists are involved individually and reflexively in the faith-based social programmes of their church. Such reflexivity leads them to self-appraise actual needs in their near environment and the way they could respond to them. From now on, not only do church leaders determine needs and actions. To do so, they rely on their soldiers. In fact, needs and adequate skills are suggested by the bottom of the organisation. These actions are totally decentralised to the individual and full consent is given. They work on the basis of a participative democracy (see Uddin and Hopper 2001). In fact, the Salvation Army operates as the frame and as the label under which soldiers operate. On the other hand, soldiers account for their involvement provisionally. The actions that they would undertake as well as the quantitative involvement therein are records of the application of their faith. Thus, the Actions Hope project leads Salvationists to self-record their Faith and Action account. Their reflexive capacity, combined with faith, leads them to undertake various concrete actions. When the parish organises weekly social work activities, soldiers are accounted for as registered volunteers.

> After the service, we all are queuing. Everybody stops for a couple of seconds in front of a blackboard and write things on it.
>
> Now, it is my turn. I approach the blackboard. I can see the scheduled activities for the week. They are exactly what was announced in the course of the service. They are arrayed with timetables (day of the week and time). In the middle there is room for people to fill in all blank cells.
>
> I fill in mine: two hours of English courses for advanced speakers on Tuesday, one hour Bible study on Thursday and two hours of music classes on Saturday. I must confess that I leave the cell for soup distribution blank that week.

Soldiers' registration for social work activities rests upon their free will and their self-evaluation of what faith commands. In that respect, they subrogate God. It is the parish minister who accounts for volunteering. Salvationists register for actions and record them using time as a working unit. The table of every week evidences how much people have volunteered. The consolidation of all weekly tables highlights the periodicity and the scope of volunteering. It becomes possible to sort the accounts by action or by individual. Hence, the total involvement of every single soldier can be appraised. The Swedish Secretary for Social Work's remark below instances this.

> As a soldier of the Salvation Army, you must be involved in our social work. How can you pretend that you are a faithful soldier and that you love your neighbour, if you do not participate in soup distribution? I know that you have plenty of time to devote to set your faith into actions. Go and get registered for the one or the other activity of the week.

Moreover, the publicity of the registration allows that the others see what faith orders. In fact, social controls frame the believer's free will. It sometimes happens that another churchgoer comments on the involvement of someone. This happened to me one day.

> I am sitting in the underground. Suddenly, someone sits beside me and greets me.
>
> 'Hi Vassili. Where are you going?'
>
> 'I am going to a swimming training session.'
>
> 'You have time for that … I noticed that you did not get registered for any activity this week. I think you should make an effort to have time for this too.'

In the incident above, the social control worked. My faith did not command anything (or I did not want to do anything). As the registration was made public, people were able to see that I did not. They then remarked on it! If soldiers volunteer out of any institutional framework, they report to their minister what they did in the week. There is no other possible control than trust in the soldier's fairness—it is assumed that his faithfulness makes him tell the truth. If he does not, it is a matter between him and God, the minister is not concerned.

> Minister's office, Paris Cœur de Vey, every Thursday, 2005–2007, 8:00 p.m.
>
> 'Hi Vassili'
>
> 'Hi Major'
>
> The minister: 'So, what did you do this week?'
>
> Me: 'Well, I participated in some of the scheduled activities, as you know. On Wednesday, I supervised for two hours the homework of a teenager.'
>
> The minister: 'What topics?'

Me: 'This week, we prepared an examination in Russian and in English. We also made several math exercises on the Thales theorem.'

Meanwhile, his spouse wrote in a book exactly what I was saying.

The Salvationist self-accounts for his involvement in social work actions. In that respect, he does like other congregation members. Whereas members of the Iona Community report their accounts to the superintendent, the Salvationist reports them directly to the minister. In the Iona Community, the believer self-accounts for his activities in a pre-established format, but the Salvationist reports them orally. The minister interrogates him and then records them in the format of the Salvation Army. The incident above demonstrates that the questions asked are to appraise the actuality and the fairness of the reporting.

To some extent, controls are consented to, insofar as the believer speaks on his or her own. The oral discursive form makes controls less formal and diachronic conversations operate as a consultative democracy (Parker 2001). However, the minister's spouse formalises the utterances of the soldier. She practices a form of bookkeeping wherein she formalises these, and so the informal conversation is translated into accounting numbers. Formalisation makes them systematic and somehow bureaucratic. On the other hand, the discursive mode in which they operate involves the individual so that he is consulted on the accounting figures to be produced. This supports the idea of consent to controls. In brief, it is the sole responsibility of the soldier that he conducts himself fairly and as his faith would command. It is also his sole responsibility that he is fair to the minister. As all this is a very personal matter between God and himself, he demonstrates self-accountability.

Once recorded at the parish level, the accounts are then formalised and reported to the territorial headquarters and then to the international headquarters. When I verify my details in the book at the entrance of the hall, I notice that all my activities in the parish that I attend in France are listed. I guess that it is also the case for the other attendees of the meeting. As I am a soldier in France, I guess that either the territorial headquarters of France or the international headquarters reported this information to the Swiss territory. The logic of double-entry bookkeeping leads to formal accounts as in the figure below (Fig. 6.2).

	Debit	Credit
Employment	E > 0	
Volunteering	V > 0	
Faith		F > 0

Fig. 6.2 Balanced 'faith and action' account

3 Balancing Witness and Collections

Witness appears in three articles of the covenant. In the fourth article, witness is seen as maintaining Christian ideals in relationships to others. In connection to this, the eighth article specifies that it is a Salvationist's duty. The ninth article suggests practicalities for witnessing: showing the spirit of Salvationism, telling the truth about the identity and the work of the Salvation Army in any circumstances. When witnessing, the believer utters before the other 'I believe in God so, because…'

3.1 Witnessing While Doing Social Work

The most obvious occasion to witness is while doing social work. Accounting for that form of witness is delineated from accounts for physical embodiment in social work. Accordingly, Salvationists are accounted for as volunteers or employees. Either Salvationists self-account for their witnessing. Or they are accounted for as registered for a social work action. Duties are accounted for as the number of hours worked and the number of people dealt with. That form of witness is accounted for ex ante and upstream. On these occasions, Salvationists are involved with facing others, disadvantaged and needy people. On the other hand, given the large scope of services provided, the Salvation Army can cover the largest part of society. This is what the European secretary for youth at the international headquarters confessed when I met him at his dwelling:

> We need that our Salvationists do as much social work as they can. This is the primary way of witnessing of our identity and of our action. We can bring the Gospel when doing social work.

Two mechanisms can be at work at the same time. On one hand, the Salvationist can witness to the capabilities of the Salvation Army and give hope. On the other hand, they can witness to the commonalities between them and other people on the grounds of ancestry. In the first mechanism, social work itself is a witness. In fact, if its beneficiary perceives it as worthwhile, he will have a good image of the Salvation Army—the organisation can operate as that which extracted him from misery. It is plausible that he is more open to religious matters, once his situation is secured. In that respect, a retired territorial commander of the United Kingdom explains:

> You cannot speak of God with someone who is starving. First, you must feed him. Only afterwards, he can be receptive […] Very often, I met people who became receptive after the Salvation Army fed them.

To some extent, the Salvation Army can appear as the saviour of people who it has aided. The officer makes the strong assumption that in the aftermath the beneficiary would pay something back. It is assumed that the outsider is reflexively thankful to the Salvation Army for its work. This would also assume that he connects the outcome thereof to religious matters. If the beneficiary of social work is capable of such reflexivity, it is understandable that soldiers are supposed to be witnessing while they are doing it. That reflexive capability of the social outsider conveys Weberian views on Protestant theology. The territorial commander in France confirms that.

Paris: Territorial Headquarters, 14 February 2006, 8:30 a.m.

> This morning, I am having a meeting with the territorial commander. I have been reading 'Economy and Society, band 2'. When he sees that, he becomes very enthusiastic.
>
> Congratulations for your readings. The Salvation Army is Weberian. Our theology is very much indebted to his work.

Accordingly, it is very coherent with Weber's observations that in most Protestant denominations aided people would understand the presence of God. They would be thankful to God for His support and would like to pay back for it.

The second mechanism at work is connected to the history and to the composition of the Salvation Army. The secretary for compliance and monitoring at the British territorial headquarters explains that

> In our congregations, we have dynasties of Salvationists. Most of our soldiers have ancestors who knew William Booth and who contributed to the foundation of the Salvation Army. In their families, there has always been one officer of the Salvation Army.

Connected to the current composition of the Salvation Army, ancestry helps understand the involvement of White Anglo-Saxon Protestants (WASPs) in social work. Their ancestors participated in the foundation of the denomination. When the Salvation Army launched its work, it recruited new members amongst people who were previously welcomed neither into society nor in any other congregation (Booth 1890; Sandall 1947, 1950). In the vocabulary of the Salvation Army, these people 'fought' poverty and misery; they 'conducted war'. Those who were able to become social insiders won over the enemy. The others were lost. Nowadays, most soldiers are full members of society. Their involvement in the denominational social work can evidence that the Salvation Army has been efficient at making them get into society. Their families or they themselves were social outsiders and became insiders thanks to the aid of the Salvation Army. As current social workers and former social outsiders, they can witness of the work of the Salvation Army. They also witness of the identity of the Salvation Army, that is a religious denomination. They are living evidence that social work and faith in Jesus Christ can help socialise people. In sum, believing in God when benefiting from the social work of the Salvation Army can result in socialisation. Correlatively, socialisation requires the combination of both. A current minister testifies:

Paris, Cœur de Vey, 14 June 2007, 8:00 p.m.

> 'When I was 20, I was homeless. One day, I met a Salvation Army officer. I knew the Salvation Army and thought they were ridiculous. The officer

talked with me. She accommodated me and offered me a meal. Then, she supported me until I graduated in economics. At that time, I understood that God had been involved. Since then, I have done the same to other people. I have been telling them my story: "God helped me when I was in your situation. He will help you too if you want Him to."'

The legitimacy of the witness consists in that he has experienced the same situation as the outsider. If he is the offspring of a former outsider family, the story told operates like a mythology. On the contrary, if he has been a social outsider himself, the witness is autobiographical. In both cases, it consists of telling the outsider: 'thanks to God, you can get back in. I did it.' Such utterances would likely be directed at gaining new souls or new supporters to the Lord. Accounting for social work is equivalent to accounting for the biography of an individual. Salvationists are expected to share their biography with others. The assumption is that it will help convince other people who are experiencing the same things that they did.

3.2 Witnessing Before Civil Society and Accountability to Stakeholder

Witnessing before civil society is the second way of honouring the covenant. Instead of doing social work, Salvationists just demonstrate before civil society and in doing so they share their religious experience with non-Salvationists. They endeavour to give reasons either for joining or for donating. Two accountability relationships are manifested in such witnessing operations. First, they honour the covenant. Secondly, they practice accountability to civil society. In the first relation, the church subrogates God and accounts for witness. In the other case, civil society subrogates God and accounts for the persuasiveness of the witness. Accounts for witness and accounts for persuasiveness mirror each other. It is to the accountability of Salvationists that they give reasons for conduct to the church and to civil society at the same time. As a member of society, the churchgoer can witness of his religious experience and of God's love. As being part of civil society and part of the church, he can demonstrate the compatibility of that double belonging. It is accountable to him that the witness convinces civil society. In fact, the persuasiveness of the testimony is one reason that would make other members of civil society donate or even join the church. An officer enumerates the occasions for witnessing before civil society:

Paris, Boulogne-Billancourt, 5 April 2007, 2:30 p.m.

> Historically, we have demonstrated in the streets or organised open-air concerts with our brass bands. It has been made more and more difficult, because we need special authorisations from local authorities. We have also been door-to-door to tell the Gospel. But it is very constraining and frustrating when people slam their door before you. We have also sold the *War Cry* in pubs. Our audience there has decreased. What we keep on doing is to witness on the occasion of various collections campaigns.

Noticeably, soldiers participate in collective witnessing operations. Depending on the occasion, they can be registered in advance. In that case the minister accounts for their presence. Or, if relatively spontaneous, the minister accounts for their spontaneous participation. Interestingly, Salvationists rarely witness before civil society on their own. Whatever the reason for privileging collective witnessing, this makes the accounting records visible. As involved in a witness team, the Salvationist is visible. His visibility can be recorded in the books of the Salvation Army, like churchgoers were in the books of the Society of Jesus (Quattrone 2004, 2009). When subrogating God, the church accounts for witnessing as for presence. Nowadays, collection campaigns are the privileged occasions for witnessing. On such occasions, the Salvation Army can collect in the capacity of a registered charity. Just when we are leaving to collect at the Manchester City stadium, the minister confirms this.

> We can witness on the occasion of collections. In fact, like any other registered charity, we are allowed to collect in the streets. Unlike other charities, we do not only collect money; we also witness of Jesus Christ.

When actually honouring the covenant, accountability shifts from the church to civil society. New external constraints frame witnessing. The Salvationist would expectedly integrate these into his conduct. Giving reasons for conduct to civil society is what allows him to conduct himself so vis-à-vis the Salvation Army. Because he practices accountability to civil society, he may honour the covenant. Simply, he may practice accountability to God. The present section evidences how accountability to civil society is part of the Salvation Army accountability system. The incident below evidences the main issues in witnessing at collections. It draws on the very issue of accountability to external stakeholders, such as possible donors and local authorities.

Witness and Collection

Manchester City Stadium, Saturday 24 November 24 2007, 1:00 p.m.

Today, Manchester City is playing in the Barclays Premier League. There are ten of us soldiers of the Salvation Army at the stadium. We are getting prepared to collect money until the kick-off. Before going to the entrances and collecting, we stand in line in front of the minister. He checks that we all wear the uniform and that we all have our collection material. He gives us all a nominative 'allowed collector' sticker from the city council that we staple on the jacket of our uniform, in case the police patrol where we are collecting.

'Make sure that you have a nominative blue collection box and not a red one. Blue is the colour of Manchester City, whereas Red is that of Manchester United. It is better not to provoke the supporters of Manchester City.'

We also bring various newspapers, annual reports, brochures and magazines published by the Salvation Army, wherein its activities are detailed. At the same time, each of us carries a tripod with the colours of the Salvation Army, for us to be visible. Each of us goes to one entrance of the stadium.

Now it is 1:30 p.m. As we are standing at the entrances, supporters of both teams start arriving. Some of them donate. When they do, my box receives only pennies. Thirty minutes later, groups come. Sometimes, one member thereof stops and donates and then other members do too. In the last twenty minutes until the kick-off, there is a long queue at the entrance. There, almost everybody donates one pound or two.

Very quickly, I have no more printed material to offer to the visitors. Fortunately, it is the kick-off now and I can dismount the tripod and carry it back with the box to the Salvation Army van in the car park. The minister picks our material up. Once he is sitting at the wheel, he addresses us all:

'Thank you very much for collecting! I will advise you individually on how much you collected, once funds are accounted for. I will tell you how much we collected altogether as well. God bless you all! See you tomorrow!'

The minister chose to make parishioners collect at the Manchester City Stadium when the local team is playing. It is now commonplace to assume that football is part of social life in the UK and in particular in Manchester, thus the Salvation Army demonstrates its anchorage in Mancunian society. Moreover, he knows what the colours of the teams are. Using collection boxes with the colours of the local team can be a way of evidencing that the members of the Salvation Army know the customs and habits of civil society in the present context. They endeavour to convince that religiosity does not prevent them from being interested in or knowing about football.

Displaying the colours of the local team at a football game in Manchester resembles a grammar (rules and codes of conduct) and set of idioms (commonly shared meanings). In fact, it is a way of giving evidence that the Salvationist is sympathetic to the team supporter. Furthermore, the minister insists on the importance of not provoking the Manchester City supporters. It is necessary to engage him by displaying to him an image wherein he can recognise himself. As the Salvationist is collecting money, the supporter can also imagine himself in a similar situation. If he were in the situation, he would likely expect people to donate. By empathy for the other as himself, he can be led to give to the Salvation Army. Interestingly, the grammar and idioms at work in the relation between the supporter and the collector act in a reflexive manner. Witnessing is similar to giving reasons for being member of the church and then for receiving gifts. Hence, the collectors at the Manchester City Stadium are accountable to the supporter of Manchester City. As collecting money upholds God's kingdom, the Salvationist remains accountable to God for that. As the counterpart of collecting is donating, the process involves the donating other, for example civil society. As the other expects its donations to be given signification, he is in situation whereby he is demanding reasons for his own conduct. By demanding signification, the other dominates the relation to the donor. The donor as a stakeholder subrogates God.

The minister also considers the case if supporters do not recognise themselves in the collector. He takes into account the possibility that the figurative mirror does not convince the supporter. It is plausible that a common language is not always a sufficient reason for donating.

Probably, the intangibility of discourse can be problematic for some people. Therefore, the minister also suggests Salvationists providing supporters with tangible material, such as magazines, brochures, annual reports and so forth. Unlike the linguistic devices, these pieces of material do not address the commonality of the other. They are directed at his rationale for donating. Those documents are aimed at explaining what the Salvation Army is and does. By showing what the Salvation Army is, the collector demonstrates how donations can be actually utilised. If this convinces the supporter, they can then be inclined to donate. Once again, the collection team gives visitors reasons for donating. These reasons are the capability for the Salvation Army to conduct its project. Thereby, the equipped collector is a device for giving reasons to the organisation's stakeholders (e.g. its donors).

Noticeably, people tend to donate more when this is done publicly. If they give, it is likely that they have reasons for doing so. Likewise, if they do not, they probably have reasons not to. Seemingly, the publicity of the event sets people in a situation where they would be hard pressed to give reasons for not donating. It is likely that on the occasion of a football game, they do not want to legitimate their conduct instead of enjoying the afternoon at the stadium. In fact, a sort of social order or social pressure from donating group members who donate calls others for doing the same. Rather than giving reasons for not donating, they tend to conform to the implicit social rule, that is giving. Everybody's conduct is visible to all others. By counting on the social group, the Salvation Army somehow reverses the accountability relationship. From then on, the group observes and subrogates the collector. That latter is recognised as legitimate and it is legitimate to donate. If not, conduct must be justified. Civil society subrogates the church, after some of its members have donated for the denominational project.

The Salvationist is accountable to the church for witnessing of its work and to the donor for his persuasiveness. At the same time as the persuasiveness of witness is part of accountability to donors, it is part of accountability to the church. Indeed, as the outcome of witnessing is a collection, the believer is accountable to the congregation for that. Whereas witnessing is part of the accountability system of the church, the individual gives reasons for his conduct (money collection or non-collection) to the church as well as to civil society. In sum, the church and civil society subrogate God in the accountability relationship.

At the same time as collectors are accountable to civil society, they are accountable to local authorities. In fact, they are requested to staple on their uniform an 'allowed collector' sticker. They are expected to show it to policemen if necessary. To those latter, they are to give reasons for collecting at the stadium. The sticker specifies that the city council gave each of them the authorisation to collect on that day at that place. From a police viewpoint, such an authorisation from the city council is a legitimate reason for this conduct. The individual is allowed to collect for the project of the Salvation Army. Nominative stickers evidence that this particular individual is allowed to collect. It is his responsibility (not that of the Salvation Army) to show it if requested.

Upstream, another accountability relationship sheds light on further subrogations. As discussed, the Salvation Army obtains authorisations from the city council for its members to collect. The reason why it is allowed to collect is seemingly that it is a well-known registered charity. When disclosing information on its activities, the Salvation Army witnesses of its work and essence. Its capability of conducting the denominational project onwards appears as a legitimate reason for local authorities. The status of a registered charity as well as the persuasiveness of the final use of the collection can be reasons for allowing collecting. Doing so, the minister practices accountability to the local authorities of Manchester. These latter subrogate God too.

One way of honouring the covenant made with God consists of demonstrating before civil society. The Salvationist is accounted for as a participant in such operations. I deliberately did not draw on how soldiers are accounted for. I rather insisted on the accountability chain. For God's kingdom to be possible, the Salvation Army organises a system of multiple subrogations wherein the individual subrogates it in its obligations (the individual is allowed to collect on behalf of the Salvation Army) and wherein local authorities subrogate God (demanding reasons for being here, e.g. for making God's kingdom come). When accounting for witness (W2), the Salvation Army accounts for all these subrogations.

3.3 Witnessing While Wearing the Uniform

Soldiers are expected to wear the Salvation Army uniform so as to be identifiable. It is a device of external witness. Consistent with Durkheim's (1902) views, the uniform is the external vehicle of the very identity of a group. Therefore, wearing the uniform appears as a means for witnessing thereof. The orders and regulations specify that every Salvationist is to wear the uniform when he or she represents the Salvation Army. The incident reported below evidences this.

Paris, Cœur de Vey, 10 September 2006

> The brass band is about to start playing while service attendees enter the hall. The twenty musicians are wearing their uniforms. The bandmaster argues with one of them who is not.
>
> 'I am sorry, son; you may not play or sing with us if you do not wear your uniform. Imagine that non-Salvationists come. What would they see if you do not wear your uniform? It is not a fair image of the Salvation Army.'

When supposed to be wearing the uniform, Salvationists are accounted for as doing or not doing. In the incident above, there is an account for not-wearing the uniform and for not witnessing. The minister writes in a book whether a soldier wears it or not.

Paris, Cœur de Vey, 7 January 2007, 12:30 p.m.

> The service is over. I am in the minister's office. His spouse nervously looks for an item in the room. After a couple of minutes, she asks me:
>
> 'Vassili, did you see my red book? I noted who was not wearing the uniform today. I must report the names in my book of account. On every occasion, I account for attendees. When I notice that there are soldiers who do not wear the uniform, I write their names. You know, they do not honour the soldier's covenant [...] This allows knowing who actually witnesses and who does not [...] By the way, you are not wearing it today".

Wearing the uniform confirms the Salvation Army's specifics to other people. Someone who does not wear it cannot display a fair image of the Salvation Army. A group uniform allows one to see who does what in society. It allows that given actions be ascribed to the right group. On the other hand, the amount of uniforms seen can be informative about the size of the group. This means that its identity and its programmes have convinced (attracted) more people than smaller ones. It can be a sign of seriousness or quality. In fact, as a minister confirms,

> Historically, the uniform of the Salvation Army has been regarded as our labour suit. Like workers have had blue collars, Salvationists have worn a uniform.

As the Salvationists' labour suit, the uniform relates to social work. It means that the soldier is *on duty*. He is available for social work or for any kind of support. The uniform actually means that the Salvation Army is present here and now. To some extent, the uniform witnesses of the Salvation Army's witnessing. Therefore, wearing it is of importance. Those who wear it are likely to do social work, while others remain anonymous and may not be involved in any social work action. In that respect, a soldier witnesses of her experience:

> Yesterday, I was staying in front of the Galeries Lafayette. I was wearing my uniform. Suddenly, someone came to me and told me: thanks to the uniform, I recognised the Salvation Army. Please, where can I oversleep next night? [...] Thanks to the uniform, I was able to advise someone. People follow the uniform of the Salvation Army. Halleluiah!

At the same time as it displays the image of the group, the uniform accompanies standardised gestures and behaviours. In order for the signification of the uniform to be externally understood, any gestures and any conduct were codified too. Consequently, the uniform also standardises people. Every single person is one piece of the whole, and standardisation aims at socialising people. No originality is allowed. Consistent with the need for the regular wearing of the uniform, I was convinced of being undisciplined the brass band conductor remarks just before the service commences once on Sunday.

> Vassili! When you are here on Sunday, you do have to wear your uniform. I know you: no red shoes, no pink tie, no purple shirt; but black shoes, white shirt and the Salvation Army tie and jacket!

The three forms of witness are associated with the collection of new souls or of new supporters. Obviously, Salvationists witness for gaining souls or monies for God's kingdom cometh.

3.4 Accounting for Witnessing and Collections

This section focuses on how the gaining of souls and of funds is accounted for. Given the coherence of the accountability system of the Salvation Army, the same logic of double-entry bookkeeping applies. Actors, procedures, evaluation models and controls are somehow the same as for the Faith and Action account.

Paris, Boulogne-Billancourt, 24 March 2007, 8:00 p.m.

> Tonight, the Boulogne-Bilancourt parish is hosting the monthly youth meeting of the Parisian Salvation Army. People between fifteen and 30 years of age are gathered for the evening. We are about 80 young people of all ages. Tonight, the topic is specifically on witness.
>
> The secretary for youth opens the session.
>
> 'Let's see if you met the targets set last time. How many of you are coming with new people? Welcome to all new comers. Please, raise your hands. Well, there are only ten new people. The challenge has not been met. Hopefully, you do better next time.'
>
> The assistant of the secretary then explains the programme of the evening. There will be workshops and plenary sessions on the definition, the finalities and the practicalities of witness.
>
> Why shall we witness? He asks.
>
> One teenager responds instantly: 'To gain new souls to the Lord and to receive monies to make His kingdom come!'
>
> 'Right, now make five-people groups and discuss these issues. Then, you will come onto the stage to present your conclusions on the practicalities and on the finalities of witness.'
>
> As I am the eldest of my workshop, I am commissioned as the secretary. In that capacity, I do not participate in the discussions. I only synthesise and write down what is said. The conclusions of the discussions are that witness consists of speaking about God with other people. Those can be schoolmates, people in the streets, borough neighbours or people cared for while volunteering. As often as possible, wearing the uniform is seen as a device for witness.

> During the plenary session, I present our results. Other non-teenagers do the same for their own group. Our conclusions are very similar. The Secretary for youth then speaks again.
>
> 'Thank you very much. You did a good work. Now, do not forget that there is no unique way of witnessing. It depends on the person who faces you. Remember Paul's epistles. Next time, your challenge is to test your witness. Bring one new person to our next meeting in two months' time.'

The incident described above evidences that witness is not gratuitous. The very issue revealed here lies in increasing the amount of souls to the Lord as well as the amount of monies devoted to the accomplishment of God's kingdom (Berry 2005; Parker 2001; Quattrone 2004). As the offspring of actions (witness), new souls and monies are considered as the net income of thereof. They increase God's properties. As such, they are accounted for as credit. On the other hand, witness is what believers do for God's kingdom. As such, they can be considered debit records. The evaluation of both credit and debit records is likely not as problematic as in the case of the Faith and Action account. Indeed, they are tangible, visible and subject to memory. As such, they can be accounted for unambiguously.

All this confirms the content of witness: it consists of sharing one's religious experience either on the occasion of social work activities, or on a discursive mode with other actors of civil society. Either way, it rests on the wearing of the uniform. Like for social work, actions can be measured in qualitative (type of witness) and in quantitative (how much time, how long, etc.) terms. As for actions, accounting figures can stem from de facto involvement noticed by the territorial headquarters, from registration as well as from self-reporting.

When doing social work, soldiers are de facto witnessing to outsiders. The nature as well as the quantitative dimension of witness is known. In fact, they are linked to the involvement in the balancing of the Faith and Action account. In such cases, witness is measured per se as the overall actions of the former account. The secretary for volunteering in France confirms this issue:

> Our soldiers are de facto registered as volunteers. When they are involved in social work actions, these are de facto accounted for witness.

Witness appears as a feature of social work. As such, it just refers to the Faith and Action account. The evaluation of witness is made at the territorial headquarters. Controls are centralised there. It also happens that soldiers are expressly called for witness actions. In that case, they must get registered like for social work actions, as the incident below outlines.

Paris, Cœur de Vey, 27 May 2007, 12:00 p.m.

The service is about to finish. Suddenly, the minister makes an extraordinary announcement.

'Today, the band is playing in front of Notre Dame. We need you for witnessing when they are playing. For further instruction, come to my office after the service. I will explain you how to get registered for the operation.'

After the service, I enter the office of the minister in order to get registered for the witness action. He writes my name in his book. I can see a column with the date and the action. My name and that of others appear in the next column.

When the congregation organises witness actions, soldiers are invited to manifest themselves and to get registered. Unlike social work actions, these take place casually. Therefore, the registration process is somewhat different from that at work for social work activities. In fact, it is the minister himself who registers people. Controls are then centralised at that level. As there is no publicity, social controls cannot apply before the event actually takes place. Then, other churchgoers can remark that someone was not present. Social controls could work afterwards, whereas the minister can exert his hierarchic control immediately. Then, attendance of the event is accounted as for witness.

Lastly, individual witness is subjected to the regular appraisal of the minister. Like for individual social work actions, the soldier is to report every week on his witness actions. At one of our weekly meetings, I report my witness actions.

I gave an examination to students of mine. It was on the introduction of management control systems in the Salvation Army. I exposed in the subject what the actions of the Salvation Army are. Namely, I could insist on the religious foundations thereof and on the linkages between the denomi-

> nation and the charity. I did not share any religious experience. Nonetheless, I witnessed of the identity of the Salvation Army.
>
> Meanwhile, the minister's spouse records in her book what I am saying. Beside some other names, I can read actions. Others are still blank.

As for individual social work actions, the soldier self-reports his witnessing to the minister. Again, controls are decentralised from the territorial headquarters and recentralised at the minister level. Again, they rely on the fairness of the churchgoer who is consulted before his actions are recorded. Regardless of actions, the records for collections are more obvious. This entire story suggests that collected souls introduce themselves. Since they are recorded as new souls when coming to a meeting, they are made visible. For that reason, the evaluation model is less problematic as in the case of faith. The visibility of the item to be recorded makes it actual and recordable (Quattrone 2009). Apparently, new people accompanying soldiers are assumed as the exact counterpart of witness. Therefore, they are systematically asked the following question:

> With whom are you coming? What is your name?
>
> Then, the name of the witness as well as the new soul is recorded in the book of the minister.

In that case, witness is appraised thanks to its outcomes: new souls. The increase of God's net income suggests that there have been adequate actions upstream—there is no doubt. On the other hand, the capability of increasing God's net income operates as a way of measuring the performance of witness. Performing witness well results in the soldier gaining actual new souls to the Lord. Records are public, so God's net income is made public to all others. Whereas the publicity of actions in the construction of the Faith and Action account led to social controls, it is likely not the case here. Rather, the performance of some soldiers is advertised. Social controls would operate reversely qua awards. The former personal secretary of the general confirms this:

> In the Salvation Army, we like awarding people. Thereby, we show them that we acknowledge their faithful actions. Hopefully, this should give other people incentives to do the same.

When witness results in the collection of monies, these are accounted for easily too. As Quattrone (2009) suggests, money is the most visible thing in an organisation. As such, it can operate like any image and can be accounted for without any ambiguity. Hence, recording the monies collected does not raise difficulties as faith does. It is the numerical monetary expression of God's net income. The incident below extends what was observed in the Manchester City situation:

Manchester Central, 25 November 2007, 11:00 a.m.

> Before the service, the minister tells each of us how much money we individually collected at Manchester City Stadium.
>
> 'Vassili, yesterday you collected 91 pounds. Congratulations, it is a good job.'
>
> 'Thank you Major!'
>
> When leaving, I have a look on his desk. In a book, he records the name of every soldier in front of the action name (Manchester City collection, 24 November 2007). In another column, I could see the amounts collected.

Every witness is given a nominative blue box. This allowed the individuation of collection recording. As money collected results from witness actions, individuation allows appraising the quality of every single soldier. The contribution of each soldier to God's net income can be known. Reciprocally, the quality of the witness can be appraised. What is unbeknown are the criteria to assess it—I cannot say if it rests upon comparisons with the outcomes of the others, or if there are target amounts to be collected. The Salvation Army is very discreet regarding that issue—unless they do not appraise the quality of witness like they do not appraise faith. Whatever the case, they record both in a book and report it to the territorial headquarters.

The Salvation Army accounts for the increase of God's net income (collections as for credit) and for ways of doing it (witness as for debit). By their construction, credit records evidence the performance of the debit records. The value of God's kingdom increases because of witness. Similarly, the integration of subrogations into witness evidence how witness contributes to the increase of God's value. The figure below summarises the appearance of the comprehensive Witness and Collections account. Zero collections would mean either inexistent or underperforming witness. Negative

	Debit	Credit (God's net income)
Social Work	W1 > 0	
Demonstrations before civil society	W2 > 0	
Uniform	W3 > 0	
Collection of souls		C1 > 0
Collection of supports (monies)		C2 > 0

Fig. 6.3 Balanced 'witness and collections' account

collections would mean that Salvationists counter witness and lost souls to the Lord. Doing so, they would decrease His net income and resources. Negative witness would result in negative collections (Fig. 6.3).

Conclusion

As in Judaism (Sombart 1911), Islam (Iqbal 1997; Taqi-Usmani 2002) or Roman Catholicism (Aho 2005; Hoskin and Macve 1986; Quattrone 2004, 2009) and to a lesser extent like the Jehovah's Witnesses (Beckford 1978), the Salvation Army accounts for what counts. Accountability leads to a managerial accounting spirituality. Every single item related to God's kingdom is accounted for credit, inasmuch as the believer is everlastingly indebted to God for those. Faith, which is difficult to appraise, is accounted for credit. So are collections of new souls and of new financial supports. Theologically speaking, faith is a manifestation of divine grace. Collections are the resources of God on earth. They are the manifestation of His kingdom. On the other hand, conduct is the manifestation of the indebtedness to God's blessings. This evidences how the believer utilises God's gifts (faith) and how they contribute to His kingdom (collections). Accordingly, actions, witness and donations are accounted for as debit.

It is difficult for faith to be appraised and measured, inasmuch as it exists within the very intimacy of the self. Is it the private gateway between the believer and God. Accordingly, it is subjected to self-appraisal and self-accounting. Nonetheless, faith is appraised in its offspring. In accordance with the Salvation Army theology, it is appraised through faithful conduct. Such conduct can be regarded as actual embodiment in the social programmes of the congregation and in donations. Embodiment in social work consists of working as a full-time employee or as a part-time volunteer. Faith can also be appraised in Sunday donations, responses to appeals and in legacies that Salvationists may make.

Employment is regarded as the labour contract connecting the soldier to the Salvation Army. This is a legal commitment that comes in addition to the initial covenant. It is expressed in terms of occupation and duties. As a full-time commitment, its features are not very much developed in the doctrines of the Salvation Army. However, volunteering is. It is expected that soldiers will register for social work operations. In practical terms, they provisionally account for time spent doing specific social actions. Afterwards, they self-report to their minister what they have actually done. Faithfulness can be appraised as the consistency of actual involvement with provisional commitment. The numerical representation of volunteering is expressed in weekly hours.

Witness is considered as the interplay between social work, demonstrations before civil society and the wearing of the uniform. When working or volunteering for social programmes, soldiers are de facto accounted for as witnesses. They share their religious journey and conceptions of the Salvation Army actions and identity with social outsiders. When witnessing before civil society, they register for specific operations and are accounted as present. Finally, when they are supposed to represent the Salvation Army, they shall wear the uniform. The minister ensures that they do so and marks those who do not. These people are then summoned.

It is expected that witnessing should result in new people joining the Salvation Army or donating for its work. In both cases, the soldier has performed well, for he has convinced them. New souls to the Lord are people who have adhered to the possibility of a double membership in the Salvation Army and in society. Social outsiders would admit that faith heuristically supports social work in order that they get into society. Social insiders would notice that it is possible to belong to civil society and to the Salvation Army. The gateway between both would be faithful conduct. When joining, these people self-account: they declare who made them come. Hence, the efficiency of the witness can be appraised ex post. New financial supporters are donors and their donations are expressed in monetary terms. They are then ascribed to one witness or another. Again, their performance can be appraised ex post.

Bibliography

Aho, J. (2005). *Confession and bookkeeping—The religious, moral, and rhetorical roots of modern accounting*. New York: State University of New York Press.

Allahyari, R. A. (2000). *Visions of charity: volunteer workers and moral community*. Los Angeles: University of California Press.

Beckford, J. A. (1978). Accounting for conversion. *The British Journal of Sociology, 29*(2), 249–262.

Berry, A. (2005). Accountability and control in a cat's cradle. *Accounting Auditing and Accountability Journal, 18*(2), 255–297.

Boltanski, L., & Chiapello, E. (1996). *Le nouvel esprit du capitalisme*. Paris: La Découverte.

Booth, W. (1890). *In darkest England and the way out*. International Headquarters of the Salvation Army, London.

Bourguignon, A., & Chiapello, E. (2005). The role of criticism in the dynamics of performance evaluation systems. *Critical Perspectives on Accounting, 16*(6), 665–700.

Brigou, D. (1994). *La Maison du Partage*. Yens sur Morge: Cabédita.

Coutts, F. (1973). *The history of the Salvation Army, vol. 6: The better fight, 1914-1946*. London: Thomas Nelson and Sons.

Coutts, F. (1986). *The history of the Salvation Army, vol. 7 : The weapons of goodwill, 1946-1977*. London: Hodder and Stoughton.

Durkheim, E. (1902). *Division of labour in society* (K. A. Fields, Trans. 1984 ed.). London: Free Press.

Hoskin, K. W., & Macve, R. H. (1986). Accounting and the examination: A genealogy of disciplinary power. *Accounting Organizations and Society, 11*(2), 105–136.

Howson, K. (2005). The Salvation Army: Aspects of their financial administration: Success and failure. *Managerial Auditing Journal, 20*(7), 649–662.

Iqbal, Z. (1997). Islamic financial systems. *Finance and Development, 34*(2), 42–45.

Irvine, H. (1999). *Who's counting? An institutional analysis of expectations of accounting in a nonprofit religious/charitable organization within a changing environment*, Unpublished PhD dissertation, University of Wollongong.

Irvine, H. (2003). Trust me! A personal account of confidentiality issues in an organisational research project. *Accounting Forum, 27*(1), 111–131.
Irvine, H. (2005). Balancing money and mission in a local church budget. *Accounting Auditing and Accountability Journal, 18*(2), 211–237.
Irvine, H., & Gaffikin, M. (2006). Getting in, getting on and getting out: Reflections on a qualitative research project. *Accounting Auditing and Accountability Journal, 19*(1), 115–145.
Jacobs, K. (2005). The sacred and the secular: Examining the role of accounting in the religious context. *Accounting Auditing and Accountability Journal, 18*(2), 189–210.
Jacobs, K., & Walker, S. P. (2004). Accounting and accountability in the Iona Community. *Accounting Auditing and Accountability Journal, 17*(3), 361–381.
Joannidès, V. (2012). Accounterability and the problematics of accountability. *Critical Perspectives on Accounting, 23*(3), 244–257.
Kreander, N., McPhail, K., & Molyneaux, D. (2004). God's fund managers: A critical study of stock market investment practices of the Church of England and UK methodists. *Accounting Auditing and Accountability Journal, 17*(3), 408–441.
Larsson, J. (2002a). Orders & regulations for corps officers of the Salvation Army, London: Salvationist Publishing.
Larsson, J. (2002b). Orders & regulations for soldiers of the Salvation Army. London: Salvationist Publishing.
Larsson, J. (2002c). Orders & regulations for territorial commanders and chief secretaries of the Salvation Army. London: Salvationist Publishing.
Laughlin, R. (1988). Accounting in its social context: An analysis of the accounting systems of the Church of England. *Accounting Auditing and Accountability Journal, 1*(2), 19–42.
Laughlin, R. (1990). A model of financial accountability and the Church of England. *Financial Accountability and Management, 6*(2), 93–114.
Lightbody, M. (2000). Storing and shielding: Financial management behaviour in a church organization. *Accounting Auditing and Accountability Journal, 13*(2), 156–174.
Lightbody, M. (2003). On being a financial manager in a church organisation: Understanding the experience. *Financial Accountability and Management, 19*(2), 117–138.
Parker, L. D. (2001). Reactive planning in a Christian bureaucracy. *Management Accounting Research, 12*(3), 321–356.
Quattrone, P. (2004). Accounting for god: Accounting and accountability practices in the Society of Jesus (Italy, XVI-XVII centuries). *Accounting Organizations and Society, 29*(7), 647–683.

Quattrone, P. (2009). Books to be practiced: Memory, the power of the visual, and the success of accounting. *Accounting, Organizations and Society, 34*, 85–118.

Quattrone, P., & Hopper, T. (2005). A 'time-space odyssey': Management control systems in two multinational organisations. *Accounting Organizations and Society, 30*(7–8), 735–764.

Raymond, A. (1976). "I fear god and honour the king": John Wesley and the American revolution. *Church History, 45*(3), 316–328.

Salvation-Army. (2010). The Salvation Army responds to Haity earthquake. Retreived from http://www.salvationarmy.org/ihq/news/3BA710B2E3E57078802576AA004D0ED3

Salvation-Army. (2012). *Annual review (2011)*. London: The Salvation Army Publishing.

Sandall, R. (1947). *The history of the Salvation Army, vol. 1: 1865-1878*. London: Thomas Nelson and Sons.

Sandall, R. (1950). *The history of the Salvation Army, vol. 2: 1878-1886*. London: Thomas Nelson and Sons.

Sandall, R. (1955). *The history of the Salvation Army, vol. 3: Social reform and welfare work*. London: Thomas Nelson and Sons.

Sombart, W. (1911). *The Jews and modern capitalism*. Kitchener, ON: Batoche Books Limited.

Taqi-Usmani, M. (2002). *An introduction to Islamic finance (Arab and Islamic laws)*. Boston, MA: CQ Press.

Thompson, G. (1991). Is accounting rhetorical? Methodology, Luca Pacioli and printing. *Accounting Organizations and Society, 16*(5–6), 572–599.

Uddin, S., & Hopper, T. (2001). A Bangladesh soap opera: Privatisation, accounting, and regimes of control in a less developed country. *Accounting Organizations and Society, 26*(7–8), 643–672.

Walker, P. J. (2001). *Pulling the Devil's kingdom down: The Salvation Army in Victorian Britain*. Los Angeles: University of California Press.

Watson, B. (1964). *A hundred years' war: The Salvation Army, 1865-1965*. New York: Hodder & Stoughton.

Weber, M. (1922). *Economy and Society*. Berkeley: The University of California Press.

Wiggins, A. R. (1960). *The history of the Salvation Army, vol. 4: 1886-1904*. London: Thomas Nelson and Sons.

Wiggins, A. R. (1968). *The history of the Salvation Army, vol. 5: 1904-1914*. London: Thomas Nelson and Sons.

Winston, D. (2000). *Red-hot and righteous: The urban religion of the Salvation Army*. Boston, MA: Harvard University Press.

7

Conclusion

It becomes clear from previous chapters that, whatever religion is in question, its linkages to accounting can be theorised in broad terms, which leaves us with a number of lessons to be learnt and opens up many research areas.

1 Theorising Accounting and Religion

Traditionally, religious accountability is directed at the Lord Himself (Weber 1922), the church building being a place 'where all authority comes from God [...] The primary accountability of a Christian is to God and is a matter of theological beliefs and conscience' (Berry 2005, p. 263). In fact, the self cannot know his Higher-Stakeholder (God, see Laughlin 1990) and can only imagine and represent Him through various pictures, whereof the Other can be part: 'when I speak to a Christian, the relation to God is presented as a relation to another person. It is not a metaphor: in the other, there is a real presence of God' (Lévinas 1991, p. 94).

All these temporal representations conflate faith (beliefs), imagination (approximations), values and norms in substitutive conduct vis-à-vis God throughout the accountability relation. Actually, church leaders and members, stakeholders and the self, demand accounts in lieu of Him,

V. Joannidès de Lautour, *Accounting, Capitalism and the Revealed Religions*, DOI 10.1007/978-3-319-32333-6_7

subrogation being manifested as 'substitution for another, one in the place of another, expiation' (Lévinas 1974, p. 15). The believer knows neither God nor His expectations and can at best approximate them by faith, which is his private matter. Ontological limitations apply to other account demanders as they do to him: his approximations are subjected to further calculations by others, the essence never being grasped but always approached (Derrida and Wieviorka 2001). At best, various approximations can converge in cascade and form a 'juxtaposition of [...] knowledges' (Hopwood 1990, p. 83), namely one by subrogator. Hence, to three realms for accounting and accountability can correspond three forms of God subrogation: the self in the divine, churchgoers and leaders in the private sphere and civil society in the public.

1.1 On the Self Subrogating God in the Divine Realm

In the divine realm, accountability is driven by faith, the believer being the right substitute for the Higher-Stakeholder qua his first interlocutor: when I am speaking to myself, I am speaking to God. Hence,

> why do we give an account to the other? Because we have something to say. But why is this known or represented something said? And even so the recourse to signs does not necessarily presuppose this communication. It can be justified by the necessity the ego finds—in its solitary synthesis of apperception—of giving signs to itself, before speaking to anyone else. [...] One can thus even write for oneself [...it] remains a 'dialogue of the soul with itself, proceeding by questions and answers' (Lévinas 1987, p. 100).

Self-accountability consists of conducting oneself consistently with one's approximation of God's will, nobody interfering in the divine realm between the Lord and the individual. As accounts are directed at everyone interested in them, their author, qua the first reader, appraises them. Thereby, he approximates his prior calculations one more time as with those of anyone else, to appraise consistency of conduct with these. In fact, such a reflexive basis makes him practice accountability to oneself and subrogate God qua an account demander.

Jacobs and Walker (2004) examine how individuals actualise the accounting and accountability rules developed by the Iona Community. There, every community member self-accounts for daily conduct and appraises consistency with what their faith commanded. In particular, individual financial stewardship and responsible self-management for the accomplishment of God's kingdom should instance self-accountability. Indeed, every member constructs his personal budgets and manages money consistently with what God could have commanded. Obviously, they cannot know His actual expectations and imagine what they could do to conduct themselves fairly. This is self-accountability, as nobody but them may access their beliefs and sense of fairness and appraise consistency of conduct with their representations of God's will. In fact, the main characteristic of accountability in a church setting is that it is an individualised practice, only the self being responsible for its accountability. Although people's fairness can be neither appraised nor controlled, others can observe its manifestations. Thus, self-accountability is restricted through the imposition of formal accounts visible to others.

Nobody can assess his/her involvement in the ontological manifestation of God's kingdom and the trustworthiness of the reasons he can give for his conduct. Nonetheless, others can observe the compliance of the self's conduct with the declaration made when the covenant was signed. Although they are capable of demanding reasons for conduct on the basis of the covenantal subrogation of God, they cannot appraise the believer's faithfulness. In that respect, in line with Jacobs and Walker (2004), the self's accountability for God's kingdom consists of being able to legitimate the conformity of its conduct with what it thinks to be His expectations and requirements. As legitimation is made on the basis of the approximation of the official signification, the believer subrogates the church that was originally subrogating God.

Consistent with Protestant perspectives on individual relationships to God, the self subrogates God too. Given the supremacy of the individual in making God's kingdom come, the individualising form of accountability is seemingly the most accurate. In distinction, the socialising one, as expressed by the denominational approximation of God's kingdom, is less visible and remains subordinated. In sum, the individual is accountable to God for working on His kingdom on earth, without the church really being able to interfere in that relationship. At best, the organisation can draw a path with clear milestones for the individual. As Lévinas (1969, 1985) suggests, individual religious experiences are the ethical and moral manifestation of the self's culture.

Only the self knows of what its religious experience consists: ontological limitations apply to all others. For that reason, the way drawn by the church informs the believer on other approximations of God. From that perspective, the individual is accountable to God for following or applying the way drawn by the church as a component of its religious experience and belief system. In this capacity, it supposedly appropriates the official approximation of God's kingdom. Its own ontological limitations then lead it to approximate the denominational approximation at the same time as God's kingdom. Hence, as the combination of various approximations, faithfulness and faithful conduct are only the fact of the believer. Precisely that mélange outlines how the self subrogates God and the church.

The accountability system of a church is directed both at God as the finality and at the self as His privileged subrogator. However, the church subrogates God by giving the covenant a normative signification whereby the believer abides. Thanks to their capacity as signification makers, church leaders dominate the organisation and are made legitimate as demanders of reasons for conduct. Whereas the accountability system is based upon a covenant made by the self with God, the church interferes by signifying and dominating the devices of the individual's religious experience.

1.2 On the Church Subrogating God in the Private Realm

The private realm is that of the fraternity, where the believer is to give accounts for conduct to church members and leaders. As he lives within a religious community, he must demonstrate conduct of consistency with the common approximations of God's will manifested in the congregation 'theology in the guise of ontology' (Cohen 1985, p. 1). Theology appears as a substitute overwhelming churchmen's ontological limitations.

Indeed, it posits a congregation's approximations as the community truth about God with which conduct must be consistent. God subrogation by the church leaves little room to self-accountability:

> The individual opens himself up to human place in terms of state, institutions, politics. Even the authority of the religious is imposed through theologies, in the truth of Reason, in the freedom of the *I* (Lévinas 1991, p. 163).

Although accountability is driven by God and practiced by faith, others subrogate Him and the believer through theologies. Indeed,

> the other in the same is my substitution for the other through responsibility, for which I am summoned as someone irreplaceable [...] The overdetermination of the ontological categories is visible, which transforms them into ethical terms. In this most passive passivity, the self liberates itself ethically from every other and from itself. Its responsibility for the other, the proximity of the neighbor, does not signify a submission to the non-ego; it means an openness in which being's essence is surpassed in inspiration (Lévinas 1974, pp. 114–115).

Ministers are legitimate subrogators of God, because, qua scientists of His speech, they are in great proximity to Him, allowing them to approach His essence.

> Proximity, as the 'closer and closer', becomes the subject. It attains its *superlative* as *my* incessant restlessness, becomes unique, then one, forgets reciprocity [...] Proximity is the subject that approaches and consequently constitutes a relationship in which I participate as a term, but where I am more, or less, than a term [...] The representation of signification itself born in the signifyingness or proximity in the measure that a third party is alongside the neighbor. [...] Proximity does not resolve into consciousness a being would have of another being that it would judge to be near inasmuch as the other would be possible for one to take hold of that being, hold on to it or converse with it, in the reciprocity of handshakes, caresses, struggle, collaboration, commerce, conversation. (Lévinas 1974, pp. 82–83)

In the capacity of scientists of God, clergy members exert hierarchical control over selves, while church members impose social controls (Jacobs and Walker 2004; Latour 2002; Parker 2001). Both forms of control (vertical and lateral) are the ontology of accounts directed at the private realm and express a dual subrogation of God by the church. Quattrone (2004, 2009) evidences vertical controls in a study of accounting and accountability in the Society of Jesus, while Jacobs and Walker (2004) demonstrate the functioning of lateral controls in the Iona Community. Contradistinctively, Quattrone (2004, 2009) reasons that church accountability is a substitute to God accountability, because the believer cannot know the Lord and therefore practice accountability to Him. Hence, church hierarchy serves as the accountability driver in this world. In fact, the Society of Jesus was structured as a military order to solve the ontology problem.

> Thus the Jesuit members did not perform the directives of the General because they were requested to do so in the Jesuit's attempt to reduce them to God. Rather they did so because, (for example through the Spiritual Exercises), the search for God was a search for their self; and the choice of a Standard (God or Lucifer) was the enactment of their ideals, which were fused with the glory of God. Along with the *reductio ad unum*, which worked from the top to the bottom of the hierarchy, there was also a *reductio ad* simple (another unity, but constituted this time by the each individual Jesuit), which worked ascending from the bottom to the top. The role played in this double reductionism by the accounting devices in use in the Society was crucial because the normative power of a 'bottom line' (Dent 1991; Law 1996) in the three systems of accountability allowed one to believe that a base had been achieved—a base, from which action was prompted. The bottom line is the ultimate point of reduction—a point that was as precarious as the self that was constructed in the Spiritual Exercises. In this sense, the Jesuit Order was the continuous and incomplete Jesuit attempt at ordering (Quattrone 2004, p. 671).

At the head was a peer-elected general, commissioning prefects in provinces. The latter were accountable to him for their jurisdiction, for example parishes, schools and homes for widows and orphans, in other words congregation operations. Beside them, procurators were commissioned to manage province resources and reported incomes and expenses to the general. Beneath them, priests were to report accounts of their flock (mainly sacraments, sins and indulgences) on a periodical basis, which appeared as the organisation memory and driver of individual and collective accountability, for

> these issues refer to the role played in the organising of our thinking by analytical methods, images, graphical, and visual representations (produced either in the mind or through writing in manuscripts and printed books). How accounting recording is intertwined with remembering seems to be a fruitful, although not yet charted territory of exploration (Quattrone 2009, p. 87).

Hence, the hierarchical structure, through accounting and vertical controls, appeared as an ontological means to hold people accountable to God for their conduct: church represented by its general in lieu of the Lord. In conclusion, vertical accountability emerged to ensure convergence of multiple interests around the absolute project of the Catholic Church through an imposed conception of God.

> It is not surprising, then, that the Benedictine father in charge of the oeconomia of the Monastery is called Padre cellerario. He is not only the one who knows how to deal with the dispensa (i.e. the cella, the pantry) but also the one who understands how to create these celles, and dispose entries into them in a meaningful manner that is useful to the multifaceted and changing activities of the Monastery (Quattrone 2009, pp. 97–98).

Jacobs and Walker (2004) show how lateral accountability and controls in the Iona Community reveal God subrogation by congregation members. Actually, every community member keeps a personal book daily with all his actual and forecasted incomes and expenses. For their personal accountancy to be meaningful to the community, they send their monthly budgets and actualisations to a buddy (neighbour) in charge of monitoring them. In turn, they control the controller's accounts, everybody observing others and being observed by them. In fact, individual fairness is appraised by the *same* others acting in lieu of God—lateral accountability revealing multiple ontologies driving administrative and authoritarian representations of fairness (Law 1996; Roberts 1996). In conclusion, through lateral social controls, congregation members subrogate God in the accountability relation.

1.3 On Civil Society Subrogating God in the Public Realm

The public realm is the world in which the congregation operates, namely civil society, as devotees work on God's kingdom through societal projects: schooling trains people to social life while social work purports to socialise outsiders. Hence, a congregation operates within a territory and addresses the world qua an economic actor, as

> every practical relationship with the world is representation, and the world represented is economic. There is a universality of economic life that opens it to the life of being (Lévinas 1975, p. 166).

In the relation to economic others, accountability moves from the private to the public realm (Arendt 1961). In fact, the religious organisation is not only accountable to God directly (private realm); it becomes accountable to its external stakeholders, that is civil society (public realm). For Lévinas and Arendt, secularisation (economisation) of the sacred emphasises the impossibility to access the divine realm. Indeed, the self has no full access to the divine but only to temporal concerns: every undertaking is marked by temporality and can be the fact of secular bodies. If it is made by a congregation, it becomes sacred to religious people but remains secular to laypeople (Booth 1993; Laughlin 1988). For instance, congregations can educate children and adults, or perform social work as secular organisations do and are therefore regarded as regular charities. This allows them to collect money from the public, receive grants, legacies and government subsidies (Anheier and Salamon 1996, 1997; Collier 2005; Connolly and Hyndman 2000, 2001, 2004; Laughlin 1996). In turn, government agencies and donors demand accounts of public money use (Gray et al. 2006; Irvine 2003; O'Dwyer and Unerman

2007; Unerman and O'Dwyer 2006a, b) because their monies enable the conduct of the congregation project. Therefore, practicing accountability to civil society is part of accountability to God: stakeholders implicitly subrogate Him in the public realm.

In conclusion, accountability in a religious setting consists of giving and demanding reasons for day-to-day conduct appraised in accordance with a religious covenant made with God (divine and private realms). Reasons are given through accounting figures, which are the language of accountability. Although records are supposedly directed at God, the impossibility to know Him leads all actors to subrogate Him. First, the self (divine realm) approximates His will and conducts itself accordingly, followed by the church (private realm) exerting dual vertical and lateral controls and by civil society (public realm) demanding formal accounts of money use (Fig. 7.1).

Religion appears as the interplay between individual experience, community and doctrines based on belief systems, values and norms manifested in faithfulness. When operating within a community, it becomes a church, a denomination or a sect managed by a scientific elite (theologians qua scientists of God). These scholars define the context of giving and demanding reasons for conduct and coordinate local religious practices,

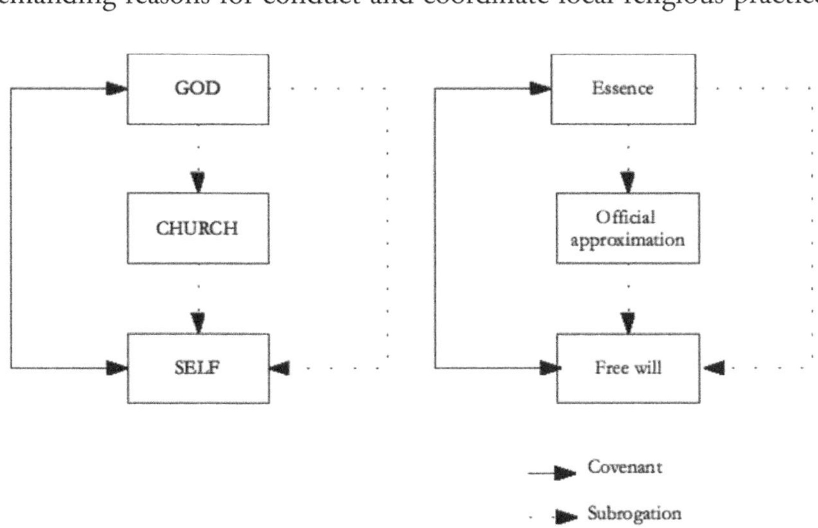

Fig. 7.1 Accountability through a cascade of subrogations

which may differ from one branch to another. Indeed, a church can be characterised by diversity.

Accountability is regarded as the interplay between demanding and giving of reasons for conduct based on common rules for justification: covenant, constitution and double-entry bookkeeping. Covenant is the mere fact of the individual who promises and declares provisional conduct, while constitution is the legal system of the community (norms). Double-entry bookkeeping, in terms of the language of accountability, is the codification of the legitimation process. In fact, accountability appears as a practice of Christian morality and entails appropriations of God's will. For ontological reasons, it can be only approximated by the self (God subrogation by the self in the divine realm), the church (vertical and lateral God subrogation by church leaders and churchgoers in the private realm) and implicitly by civil society (God subrogation by stakeholders in the public realm). In conclusion, accountability is revealed as a cascade of approximations and subrogations upheld by controls. The diagram below summarises and generalises these relationships: a unique covenant upheld by dual subrogating systems (Fig. 7.2).

In a religious denomination, as in any other organisation, a Higher-Stakeholder supplies resources. His expectations are likely that the

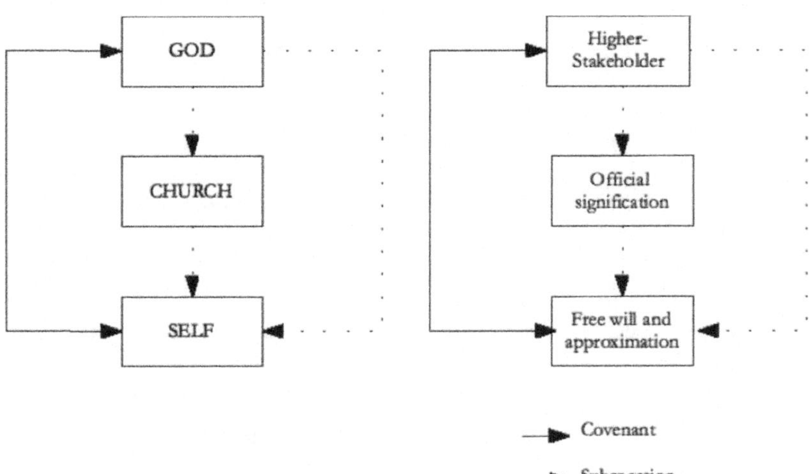

Fig. 7.2 Subrogating god with covenants

organisation uses them to perform projects that will create value, be it financial or non-financial. These counterparts are expressed in accounting figures (resources as credit equalling actions and stakeholder value as debit). The precise content of stakeholder value, given the assumption of ontological limitation, is unknown. For the organisation to be able to work on it, one signification is expected. Managers are commissioned to supply an official approximation thereof. In telling the signification, they reveal what the organisational truth and norms are (McKernan and Kosmala 2007); they ensure the domination of the organisation. Accountability rests upon the demanding (from managers) and giving (from organisational members) of legitimate reasons for conduct on the basis of the official approximation of the higher expectations. From a systematic perspective, the ontological assumption applies to the members of the organisation too. It is highly probable that the official doctrine is not totally unambiguous (Munro 1995). As they are not able to access the manager's mind, they can give to the official doctrines their own signification and legitimate their conduct accordingly. Since managers give the normative signification of Higher-Stakeholder value, they dominate the organisation and socialise its members. Managers are His main subrogator. Given the ontological assumption, organisational members do individualise accountability and subrogate both managers and the Higher-Stakeholder.

Notwithstanding similar dimensions and forms of accountability, as well as relationships involved, a church setting differentiates itself from other organisations. The case of the Salvation Army, informed with Berry's (2005) study on covenant, outlined that the commitment of the church member to the Higher-Stakeholder is explicit. In fact, the religious belief system and the integration of individual religious experiences are the basis for individual accountability. The organisation only influences the relationship. It is likely that in most organisations members are not called to make an explicit covenant with the Higher-Stakeholder. Correlatively and counterintuitively, it is likely that the exercise of the individual's free will is more possible to realise in a church setting that in other organisations. In spite of an explicit covenant, the Higher-Stakeholder's expectations as well as the official approximation thereof is more ambiguous than in other organisations. This can be attributed to the impossibility to know God, whereas a human Higher-Stakeholder can be questioned.

Different from any other organisation, where managers' legitimacy stems from their commissioning by the Higher-Stakeholder, that of those in a religious organisation is not as obvious. It is likely that they gain legitimacy by dominating the denomination.

The present chapter has been concerned about those at whom accountability is directed. The broad content of accountability allowed us to grasp that accountability practices are not only directed at stockholders. More broadly, they are directed at a Higher-Stakeholder, whoever that is (Laughlin 1996). Depending on the accountable person (Bolland and Schultze 1996), these practices can be directed either at stockholders, customers, suppliers, employees, managers, public authorities or any other interested person. Consistent with that, any actor within the organisation has an accountability role (Johansen 2008). In fact, accountability relationships evidence multiple ontologies (Law 1996). The major contribution of this book consists of the focus on the ontological issue.

In phenomenology, ontology is regarded as the study of the 'to be' and of 'being' (Arendt 1961, 1968, 1989; Lévinas 1969, 1974, 1975, 1991). Based upon Descartes', Kant's and Husserl's philosophy, ontology addresses the issue of knowledge (Law 1996): what do I know? What can I know? One major conclusion is that I do not know myself. Accordingly, I can know neither the Other nor his thought. In fact, this whole book has applied to accounting practice the traditional ontological assumptions and questionings of qualitative research. To some extent, it assumes that accountability enquiries are similar to research enquiries. Hence, its contribution to the accountability literature consists in that the accountable person cannot know the expectations of the Higher-Stakeholder.

It is commonplace to consider that the finality of the organisation is the fulfilment of the Higher-Stakeholder's expectations. Stockholders have capitalistic expectations, whereas other types of stakeholders may have non-capitalistic concerns. The understanding of the Higher-Stakeholder's expectation is not an exact science. At best, every intermediary can approximate His actual will and expectations, be they capitalistic or not. Managers are commissioned to fulfil these. As they cannot exactly know them (what quantification of actual financial expectations, for instance?), they approximate them and make of these approximations the official organisational doctrine. It is on this basis that they may demand other organisational actors' reasons for conduct. Thereby, managers become substitutes of the Higher-Stakeholder. By representing them on the basis of their own approximations, they subrogate them. Accountability is directed at them and in that capacity, they in turn become the Higher-Stakeholder of levels beneath. Hence, at every level, the present individual subrogates the Higher-Stakeholder. At the end of the chain, the employee approximates these expectations and imposes them to the inexistent inferior level. Actually, his approximation becomes his own doctrine of what the Higher-Stakeholder expects. In brief, the employee conducts himself in accordance with what his approximation orders. He is accountable to himself in order to fulfil the Higher-Stakeholder's expectations.

In the cascade of subrogations, every organisational member is accountable to all intermediary stakeholders and to themselves. Such views on accountability bring it into the field of corporate social responsibility (Chong 2005; Cooper and Owen 2007; Ezzamel et al. 2007; Gray et al. 2006; Jinnai 2005; O'Dwyer and Unerman 2007; Unerman and O'Dwyer 2007). To some extent, the ontological issue conveys accountability relationships as corporate social accountability. In the cascade of subrogations, every single intermediary stakeholder subrogates the Higher-Stakeholder. Accountability to them is part of ultimate accountability to the inaccessible Higher-Stakeholder.

It suggests that accountability is the interplay between discursive practices, accounting, controls and evaluation, that is accounterability and accounting figures. Contingency theory-based or agency theory-based literature tends to assimilate accounting and accountability. Since Roberts and Scapens (1985) grasped accountability, recent works on the subject have related it to accounting, taking the latter as its language. Individuals may be demanded to give oral reasons for conduct rather than accounting figures. This chapter reasons that accounting is a device for accountability practices but not the sole one, which leaves room for accounterability (see Kamuf 2007).

Financial accounting is not the mere language of accountability. Few works have addressed the linkages between accountability and controls (Berry 2005; Broadbent and Laughlin 2003; Ezzamel 1997; Goddard and Powell 1994; Munro 1993; Toms 2005). Whereas most of these works tend to assimilate control and accountability, only two (Berry 2005; Peace 2006) consider controls as means to appraise conduct. In both pieces of research, accountability rests upon a covenant made either by the individual with the organisation on behalf of the Higher-Stakeholder (Berry 2005) or by organisational leaders with other stakeholders (Peace 2006). In both cases, the covenant evidences that the individual promises to abide by the organisational belief system on his own. Self-control, social controls (peer controls) and hierarchical controls apply. Thus, all controls, including financial and management accounts, are accountability drivers and form altogether organisational accountability.

In that context, organising also becomes an accountability driver. Indeed, when looking for the Higher-Stakeholder and for intermediary stakeholders, the individual informs on the state of the organisation. The central issue is to identify to whom one is accountable. This sheds light on the amount and the nature of intermediaries between the very accountable individual and the Higher-Stakeholder. Seemingly, the more intermediaries, the more centralised and coercive are the controls. On the contrary, the fewer intermediaries, the more decentralised and the more negotiated are the controls. Bureaucracy, political hegemony, participative democracy and representative democracy appear as ways of organising. As these seem to drive the design of accountability systems and the practices thereof, others would assumedly do so too. We disagree with Kamuf's assertion that

> Narrative accounting and computational accounting are even commonly thought to stand in a rough opposition to each other, the former occupying a pole in the vicinity of an act of witnessing or testimony, called, very loosely, subjective, while the latter lies at or close to the pole of what counts as objective fact, evidence, or even proof (p. 252).

2 Lessons and Research Agenda

The ontological issue presented throughout this book prevents us from suggesting objective measurement systems and evaluation models, the fallacy of objective measures shedding light on ideological approximations of stakeholders' actual expectations (Bourguignon 2005; Bourguignon and Chiapello 2005). For instance, evaluation models such as the CAPM rest upon quasi-religious assumptions that investors are totally rational and that financial markets are efficient. None of those assumptions can be deemed as objective. However, they drive most accounting and accountability practices. Usually, stockholders are seeking for value maximisation, to which company workers are to contribute. In the Capital Asset Pricing Model (CAPM), stockholders supposedly know the risk/return combination of a company, risk being either financial or operational. Through financial decisions (with regard to financial structure or investment policy), managers can inflect deviations from average expectable return. On the other hand, employees have a dual accountability role (Johansen 2008), insofar as they can blend operational risk, which can ultimately alter the combination and expectations of the investor. However, investor expectations are ontologically subjected to various approximations made both by managers and employees. First, managers make their approximations the official organisational doctrine apropos the Higher-Stakeholder expectations, namely the corporate belief system from which no deviation should be tolerated. In turn, employees approximate these approximations to conduct their daily activities—convergence, coherence and congruence of conduct being enabled through controls (de Haas and Algera 2002). In the meantime, to ensure the perfect fulfilment of the Higher-Stakeholder's expectations, employees approximate these on their own. This leads them to conduct themselves in such a manner that they comply with their approximation, practicing therefore self-accountability. In each case, when explaining the very content of their approximations and conduct, they practice accounterability to the Higher-Stakeholder, the organisation and themselves. In that sense, I agree with Quattrone's (2009) statement that

> given that remembering is never a simple recollection of stored memories [...] the reader of the book always performs an appropriation of the text [...] which, it is argued later in the Section 'Accounting as a working space/time: the importance of "praxis" beyond functionalism and towards knowledge commodification' implies a modification [... of what seems to remain a stable set of prescriptions into something which is different but still the same. Beyond their persuading power, these inscriptions, these signs, can be viewed as forces, as acts and effects of engagement [...] which ignite the process of knowledge fabrication (p. 89).

Indeed,

> the secularisation of knowledge [...] entails a relationship with some shared practices (which define an organisation and a society), in order for this knowledge to exist and acquire meaning [...] This brings us back to a new form of religiosity, of liturgy, in which meaning is defined through the fulfilment of some type of devotional practice. Accounting inscriptions (in budgets, activity based costing systems, balanced scorecards, and the like) mean little if not enacted through specific orthopraxis which, in the context of this paper and early modern treatises, was related to the art of memory and rhetoric (Quattrone 2009, p. 112).

An extension to the present book would consist of applying the theoretical framework and conclusions to other organisational contexts. The application of the theoretical framework for accountability to other organisations would result in discussions about the relevance of issues related to organisational belief systems, covenants, constitutions and subrogations. This would allow theoretical refinements for increased understanding of accountability relationships.

The first lesson we can learn from this book is that research dealing with accounting and religion is mostly grounded in history and tends to be descriptive of how accounting is practiced in a particular church setting. This started with Laughlin's (1988) seminal accounting history paper. As it does seem these publications remain grounded in a conventional accounting history tradition, their authors do not sufficiently insist on what can be learnt of contemporary accounting at large or religious accounting today. In 2016, accounting history research dramatically needs papers bringing religious settings into contemporary perspectives, thereby following new accounting history recommendations.

The second lesson learnt from this book is that accounting in a particular micro setting tends to be studied at the expense of an understanding of the big picture. Such a big picture can be grasped through interdisciplinary studies borrowing from religion's home discipline. Scholars could discuss more closely the theological grounds of accounts and the rationale for giving an account. The more theologies of accounting we have, the better we can understand where denominations stand.

Thirdly, even though theologies have been discussed and explicated, such studies remain scarce and these studies have only discussed Christian theologies—most of the time Anglo-Saxon Protestant theologies and much more rarely Catholic or liberation theology. Yet, even within Christianity, numerous theologies operate. Hence, more non-Protestant theologies need to be discussed in relation to accounting, as done by Lim (2014) with Bonheoffer's approach. Secondly, mostly Christian settings in Western (Anglo-Saxon) countries have been studied, whilst the world embraces so much more. Therefore, more research on accounting and religion in other contexts would be welcome, such as developing countries, Orthodox countries or Eastern Christian countries (e.g. Lebanon or Syria). For now, Joannidès de Lautour et al. are working on a project addressing the ethnic appropriation of a British-imposed accountability system in the Salvation Army. They are looking into the way historical belief systems accommodate the one resulting from a conversion, in this case how Voodoo heritage hosts Methodist perspectives.

Finally, Islam and Judaism have received very little academic attention, even though the *Journal of Islamic Business and Accounting* was launched in 2010. More broadly, other religions, such as Animism, Buddhism or Shintoism have been neglected. Therefore, research into those non-Western or non-mainstream religions would be useful to see how far religion can influence accounting. Within each of these religions, different theological perspectives would be more than welcome, in order that academe does not unduly amalgamate different communities. For instance, Shiaism and Sunnism differ in their essence on the grounds of the Prophet's real identity (Ali or Mohammed), hence one should certainly not conflate them into one single category called Islam. Rather, research engaging more in detail in each theological perspective's influence in accounting within those other religions is needed.

Bibliography

Anheier, H., & Salamon, L. (1996). *The emerging nonprofit sector: An overview.* Manchester: Manchester University Press.

Anheier, H., & Salamon, L. (1997). *Defining the emerging sector: A cross-national analysis.* Baltimore, MD: The John Hopkins Sector Series.

Arendt, H. (1961). *The human condition.* Chicago, IL: The University of Chicago Press.

Arendt, H. (1968). *Totalitarianism: Part three of the origins of Totalitarianism*. Boston, MA: Harvest Books.

Arendt, H. (1989). *La crise de la culture*. Paris: Folio.

Berry, A. (2005). Accountability and control in a cat's cradle. *Accounting Auditing and Accountability Journal, 18*(2), 255–297.

Bolland, R. J., & Schultze, U. (1996). Narrating accountability: Cognition and the production of the accountable self. In R. Munro & J. Mouritsen (Eds.), *Accountability: Power, ethos and the technologies of managing* (pp. 62–82). London: International Thomson Business Press.

Booth, P. (1993). Accounting in churches: A research framework and agenda. *Accounting Auditing and Accountability Journal, 6*(4), 37–67.

Bourguignon, A. (2005). Management accounting and value creation: The profit and loss of reification. *Critical Perspectives on Accounting, 16*, 353–389.

Bourguignon, A., & Chiapello, E. (2005). The role of criticism in the dynamics of performance evaluation systems. *Critical Perspectives on Accounting, 16*(6), 665–700.

Broadbent, J., & Laughlin, R. (2003). Control and legitimation in government accountability processes: The private finance initiative in the UK. *Critical Perspectives on Accounting, 14*(1–2), 23–48.

Chong, G. (2005). Materiality, accountability and social responsibility. *Critical Perspectives on Accounting, 16*(1), 61–62.

Cohen, R. A. (1985). *Translator's introduction*. In E. Lévinas (Ed.), *Ethics and infinity* (pp. 1–15). Pittsburgh: Duquesne University Press.

Collier, P. M. (2005). Governance and the quasi-public organization: A case study of social housing. *Critical Perspectives on Accounting, 16*(7), 929–949.

Connolly, C., & Hyndman, N. (2000). Charity accounting: An empirical analysis of the impact of recent changes. *The British Accounting Review, 32*(1), 77–100.

Connolly, C., & Hyndman, N. (2001). A comparative study on the impact of revised SORP 2 on British and Irish charities. *Financial Accountability and Management, 17*(1), 73–97.

Connolly, C., & Hyndman, N. (2004). Performance reporting: A comparative study of British and Irish charities. *The British Accounting Review, 36*(2), 127–154.

Cooper, S. M., & Owen, D. L. (2007). Corporate social reporting and stakeholder accountability: The missing link. *Accounting Organizations and Society, 32*(7–8), 649–667.

de Haas, M., & Algera, J. A. (2002). Demonstrating the effect of the participative dialogue: Participation in designing the management control system. *Management Accounting Research, 13*(1), 41–69.

Dent, M. (1991). Information technology and managerial strategies in the NHS: Computer policies, organizational change and the labour process. *Critical Perspectives on Accounting, 2*(4), 331–360.

Derrida, J., & Wieviorka, M. (2001). *Foi et savoir*. Paris: Seuil.

Ezzamel, M. (1997). Accounting, control and accountability: Preliminary evidence from Ancient Egypt. *Critical Perspectives on Accounting, 8*(6), 563–601.

Ezzamel, M., Robson, K., Stapleton, P., & McLean, C. (2007). Discourse and institutional change: 'Giving accounts' and accountability. *Management Accounting Research, 18*(2), 150–171.

Goddard, A., & Powell, J. (1994). Accountability and accounting: Using naturalistic methodology to enhance organizational control—A case study. *Accounting Auditing and Accountability Journal, 7*(2), 50–69.

Gray, R., Bebbington, J., & Collison, D. (2006). NGOs, civil society and accountability: Making the people accountable to capital. *Accounting Auditing and Accountability Journal, 19*(3), 319–348.

Hopwood, A. G. (1990). Ambiguity, knowledge and territorial claims: Some observations on the doctrine of substance over form: A review essay. *The British Accounting Review, 22*(1), 79–87.

Irvine, H. (2003). Trust me! A personal account of confidentiality issues in an organisational research project. *Accounting Forum, 27*(1), 111–131.

Jacobs, K., & Walker, S. P. (2004). Accounting and accountability in the Iona Community. *Accounting Auditing and Accountability Journal, 17*(3), 361–381.

Jinnai, Y. (2005). Towards a dialectical interpretation of the contemporary mode of capitalist accounting. *Critical Perspectives on Accounting, 16*(2), 95–113.

Johansen, T. R. (2008). 'Blaming oneself': Examining the dual accountability role of employees. *Critical Perspectives on Accounting, 19*(4), 544–571.

Kamuf, P. (2007). Accounterability. *Textual practice, 21*(2), 251–266.

Latour, B. (2002). *Jubiler ou les tourments de la parole religieuse*. Paris: Seuil.

Laughlin, R. (1988). Accounting in its social context: An analysis of the accounting systems of the Church of England. *Accounting Auditing and Accountability Journal, 1*(2), 19–42.

Laughlin, R. (1990). A model of financial accountability and the Church of England. *Financial Accountability & Management, 6*(2), 93–114.

Laughlin, R. (1996). Principals and higher-principals: Accounting for accountability in the caring professions. In R. Munro & J. Mouritsen (Eds.), *Accountability: Power, ethos and the technologies of managing* (pp. 225–244). London: International Thomson Business Press.

Law, J. (1996). Organizing accountabilities: Ontology and the mode of accounting. In R. Munro & J. Mouritsen (Eds.), *Accountability: Power, ethos and the technologies of managing* (pp. 283–306). London: International Thomson Business Press.

Lévinas, E. (1969). *Totality and infinity*. Pittsburg: Duquesne University Press.

Lévinas, E. (1974). *Otherwise than being or beyond essence*. Pittsburgh: Duquesne University Press.

Lévinas, E. (1975). *God, death and time*. Stanford, CA: Stanford Univeristy Press.

Lévinas, E. (1985). *Ethics and infinity*. Pittsburg: Duquesne University Press.

Lévinas, E. (1987). *Time and the Other* (R. A. Cohen, Trans.). Pittsburg: Duquesne University Press.

Lévinas, E. (1991). *Entre nous: Thinking-of-the-other*. New York: Continuum.

Lim, F. (2014). *The economic entity and accounting for labour: insights from Dietrich Bonhoeffer (1906 – 1945)*. PhD, Victoria University of Wellington, Wellington, New Zealand.

McKernan, J. F., & Kosmala, K. (2007). Doing the truth: Religion—Deconstruction—Justice, and accounting. *Accounting Auditing and Accountability Journal, 20*(5), 729–764.

Munro, R. (1993). Just when you thought it safe to enter the water: Accountability, language games and multiple control technologies. *Accounting Management and Information Technologies, 3*(4), 249–271.

Munro, R. (1995). Managing by ambiguity: An archaeology of the social in the absence of management accounting. *Critical Perspectives on Accounting, 6*(5), 433–482.

O'Dwyer, B., & Unerman, J. (2007). From functional to social accountability: Transforming the accountability relationship between funders and non-governmental development organisations. *Accounting Auditing and Accountability Journal, 20*(3), 446–471.

Parker, L. D. (2001). Reactive planning in a Christian bureaucracy. *Management Accounting Research, 12*(3), 321–356.

Peace, R. (2006). Accountants and a religious covenant with the public. *Critical Perspectives on Accounting, 17*(6), 781–797.

Quattrone, P. (2004). Accounting for God: accounting and accountability practices in the Society of Jesus (Italy, XVI–XVII centuries). *Accounting, Organizations and Society, 29*(7), 647–683.

Quattrone, P. (2009). Books to be practiced: Memory, the power of the visual, and the success of accounting. *Accounting, Organizations & Society, 34*(1), 85–118.

Roberts, J. (1996). From discipline to dialogue: Individualizing and socialising forms of accountability. In R. Munro & J. Mouritsen (Eds.), *Accountability: Power, ethos and the technologies of managing* (pp. 40–61). London: International Thomson Business Press.

Roberts, J., & Scapens, R. (1985). Accounting systems and systems of accountability – understanding accounting practices in their organisational contexts. *Accounting, Organizations and Society, 10*(4), 443–456.

Toms, S. (2005). Financial control, managerial control and accountability: Evidence from the British cotton industry, 1700-2000. *Accounting Organizations and Society, 30*(7–8), 627–653.

Unerman, J., & O'Dwyer, B. (2006a). On James Bond and the importance of NGO accountability. *Accounting Auditing and Accountability Journal, 19*(3), 305–318.

Unerman, J., & O'Dwyer, B. (2006b). Theorising accountability for NGO advocacy. *Accounting Auditing and Accountability Journal, 19*(3), 349–376.

Unerman, J., & O'Dwyer, B. (2007). The business case for regulation of corporate social responsibility and accountability. *Accounting Forum, 31*(4), 332–353.

Weber, M. (1922). *Economy and society.* Berkeley, CA: The University of California Press.

Further Readings

Judaism

Attali, J. (2002). *Les Juifs, le monde et l'argent*. Paris: Fayard.
Cohen, J. (1980a). Original sin and the evil inclination: A polemicit's appreciation of human nature. *The Harvard Theological Review, 73*(3/4), 495–520.
Copeland, S. (2002). That law which calls away from mystifying rapture to religious responsibility. *Jthisnal of Law and Religion, 17*(1/2), 111–119.
Derrida, J., & Weber, E. (2004). *Questioning Judaism*. Stanford, CA: Stanford University Press.
Kaplan, L. (1998). Israel under the moundain: Emmanuel Levinas on freedom and constraint in the revelation of the Torah. *Modern Judaism, 18*(1), 35–46.
Lévinas, E. (1963). *Difficult freedom—Essays on Judaism*. Baltimore, MD: The John Hopkins University.
Neusner, J. (1979). *The way of Torah—An introduction to Judaism*. Belmont, CA: Wadsworth Inc..
Ross, J. (1999). The primacy of the personalist concept of god in Jewish thought. *The Jthisnal of Jewish Thought and Philosophy, 8*, 171–199.
Schechter, S. (1894a). Some aspects of rabbinic theology I. *The Jewish Quarterly Review, 6*(3), 405–427.
Schechter, S. (1894b). Some aspects of rabbinic theology II. *The Jewish Quarterly Review, 6*(4), 633–647.

V. Joannidès de Lautour, *Accounting, Capitalism and the Revealed Religions*, DOI 10.1007/978-3-319-32333-6

Schechter, S. (1895a). Some aspects of rabbinic theology III. *The Jewish Quarterly Review, 7*(2), 195–215.
Schechter, S. (1895b). Some aspects of rabbinic theology: The "law". *The Jewish Quarterly Review, 8*(1), 1–16.
Schechter, S. (1896). Some aspects of rabbinic theology VI. The Torah in its aspects of law. *The Jewish Quarterly Review, 8*(3), 363–380.
Sombart, W. (1911). *The Jews and modern Capitalism*. Kitchener, ON: Batoche Books Limited.
Sombart, W. (1916). *The quintessence of Capitalism*. London: T. Fisher Unwin, Ltd.
Ward, K. (1999). The god of philosophers and the god of Abraham, Isaac and Jacob. *The Jthisnal of Jewish Thought and Philosophy, 8*, 157–170.
Weber, M. (1922). *Economy and society*. Berkeley, CA: The University of California Press.

Roman Catholicism

Aho, J. (2005). *Confession and bookkeeping—The religious, moral, and rhetorical roots of modern accounting*. New York: State University of New York Press.
Case, S. (1907). Authority for the sacraments. *The BIblical World, 29*(5), 357–360.
de Certeau, M. (1986). *Heterologies: Discthisse on the other*. Minneapolis: University of Minnesota Press.
Christie, F. (1918). Church and sacraments. *The American Jthisnal of Theology, 22*(1), 143–145.
Cohen, J. (1980b). Original sin and the evil inclination: A polemicit's appreciation of human nature. *The Harvard Theological Review, 73*(3/4), 495–520.
Cohen, J. (1980c). Rational Capitalism in Renaissance Italy. *The American Jthisnal of Sociology, 85*(6), 1340–1355.
Dante. (1314). *L'Enfer*. Paris: Garnier-Flammarion.
Dante. (1316). *Le Purgatoire*. Paris: Garnier-Flammarion.
Dante. (1321). *Le Paradis*. Paris: Garnier-Flammarion.
Hallman, B. (1985). *Italian cardinals, reform and the church as property*. Los Angeles: University of California Press.
Harrison, P. (2002). Original sin and the problem of knowledge in Early Modern Europe. *Jthisnal of History of Ideas, 63*(2), 239–259.
Michaud, C. (1991). *L'Eglise et l'argent sous l'Ancien Régime—Les receveurs généraux du clergé de France aux XVIè—XVIIIè siècles*. Paris: Fayard.

Norman, A. (1997). Regress and the doctrine of epistemic original sin. *The Philosophical Quarterly, 14*(189), 477–494.
Panofsky, E. (1951). Two roger problems: The donor of the hague lamentation and the date of the altarpiece of the seven sacraments. *The Art Bulletin, 33*(1), 33–40.
Pascal, B. (1656). Ecrits sur la grâce. In B. Pascal (Ed.), *De l'esprit géométrique* (pp. 120–140). Paris: Garnier-Flammarion.
Pascal, B. (1670). *Pensées*. Paris: Garnier-Flammarion.
Quattrone, P. (2004). Accounting for god: Accounting and accountability practices in the society of Jesus (Italy, XVI–XVII centuries). *Accounting Organizations and Society, 29*(7), 647–683.
Quattrone, P. (2009). Books to be practiced: Memory, the power of the visual, and the success of accounting. *Accounting, Organizations and Society, 34*(1), 85–118.
Reinburg, V. (1992). Liturgy and the laity in late medieval and reformation France. *The Sixteenth Century Jthisnal, 23*(3), 526–547.
Saint-Augustin. (1637). *Les confessions*. Paris: Garnier-Flammarion.

Islam

Aqbal, Z., & Mirakhor, A. (2006). *Introduction to Islamic finance: Theory and practice*. London: John Wiley and Sons.
Crone, P. (2004). *Meccan trade and the rise of Islam*. Princeton, NJ: Princeton University Press.
Décobert, C. (2004). L'autorité religieuse aux premiers siècles de l'Islam. *Archives des Sciences Sociales des Religions, 125*, 23–44.
Gambling, T., & Karim, R. A. (1991). *Business and accounting ethics in Islam*. London: Continuum International Publishing.
Iqbal, Z. (1997). Islamic financial systems. *Finance and Development, 34*(2), 42–45.
Iqbal, Z., & Mirakhor, A. (2006). *Introduction to Islamic finance: Theory and practice*. London: John Wiley and Sons.
Mohammed, I. (2000). Concept of predestination in Islam and Christianity: Special reference to Averroes and Aquinas. *The Islamic Quarterly, 44*(2), 393–413.
Murata, S., & Chittik, W. (1994). *The vision of Islam*. New York: Paragon House.
Napier, C. (2009). Defining Islamic accounting: Current issues, past root. *Accounting History, 14*(1/2), 121–144.

Rodinson, M. (1966). *Islam and Capitalism*. London: Saqi Essentials.
Smith, W. C. (1957). *Islam in modern history*. New York: New American Library.
Tapper, N., & Tapper, R. (1987). The birth of the Prophet: Ritual and gender in Turkish Islam. *Man New Series, 22*(1), 69–92.
Taqi-Usmani, M. (2002). *An introduction to Islamic finance (Arab and Islamic Laws)*. Boston, MA: CQ Press.
Thomson, W. (1950a). Free will and predestination in early Islam I. *The Muslim World, 40*(3), 207–216.
Thomson, W. (1950b). Free will and predestination in early Islam II. *The Muslim World, 40*(4), 276–287.
Tinker, T. (2004). The enlightenment and its discontents: Antinomies of Christianity, Islam and the calculative sciences. *Accounting, Auditing and Accountability Jthisnal, 17*(3), 442–475.
Torrey, C. (1967). *The Jewish foundation of Islam*. Ktav Publishing Inc.
Watt, W. M. (1946). Free will and predestination in early Islam. *The Muslim World, 36*(2), 124–152.
Zubair, H. (1983). Theory of profit: The Islamic viewpoint. *Jthisnal of Research on Islamic Economics, 1*(1), 3–14.

Index

Note: Page number followed by "n" denote footnotes

V. Joannidès de Lautour, *Accounting, Capitalism and the Revealed Religions,* DOI 10.1007/978-3-319-32333-6

D

E

F

G

The manufacturer's authorised representative in the EU is Springer Nature Customer Service Centre GmbH, Europaplatz 3, 69115 Heidelberg, Germany. If you have any concerns regarding our products, please contact ProductSafety@springernature.com

Printed and bound by CPI Group (UK) Ltd, Croydon, CR0 4YY

30/09/2026

02225514-0019